CW00807399

Compassionate Caring

Compassionate Caring

A Daily Pilgrimage of Pain and Hope

Trevor Hudson

eagle

Guildford, Surrey

Copyright © 1999 Trevor Hudson

The rights of Trevor Hudson to be identified as author of this work has been asserted by him in accordance with the Copyright, Designs and Patents Act 1988.

British Library Cataloguing in Publication Data. A catalogue record for this book is available from the British Library.

Published by Eagle, an imprint of Inter Publishing Service (IPS) Ltd, PO Box 530, Guildford, Surrey GU2 5FH.

All rights reserved. No part of this publication may be reproduced or transmitted in any form or by any means, electronic or mechanical, including photocopying, recording or any information storage and retrieval system, without either prior permission in writing from the publisher or a licence permitting restricted copying.

In the United Kingdom such licences are issued by the Publishers Licensing Society Ltd, 90 Tottenham Court Road, London W1P 9HE.

Unless otherwise noted, Scripture quotations are taken from the New Standard Revised Version © 1988 Division of Christian Education of the National Council of Churches of Christ in the United States of America. (Published in the UK by HarperCollins.)

Typeset by Eagle
Printed by Bell & Bain, Glasgow
ISBN No: 0 86347 295 8

Our times cry out for a gospel-shaped spirituality that is both intensely personal and deeply aware of our suffering neighbour.

Contents

Acknowledgements

Several people encouraged me while this book gradually came to life. My deepest thanks go to the following:

- to David Wavre and Joyce Huggett for their gentle insistence that the pilgrimage experience was worth writing about, and to the editorial staff at Eagle for their skilful preparation of the final manuscript;
- to Wanda Nash for her incisive and insightful feedback on each chapter. The attention which she gave to the text was a gift of grace;
- to Bill Meaker who corrected my grammar and made numerous helpful suggestions;
- to the pilgrims themselves, and especially to Stephen Carpenter, Brian Burger, Neil and Adele Thomas, and Gavin Launders for allowing me to quote their reflections;
- to Ruth Rice for her listening companionship on my own personal pilgrimage;
- to the Sisters at St Benedicts, Rosettenville and Sister Margaret Magdalen for their faithful intercessions and supportive interest in the book;
- to Lyn Meyer for placing her computer skills so generously at the service of this book
- and lastly, to Debbie, Joni and Mark who keep loving me through thick and thin. I dedicate the book to them.

Preface

This is a book with a difference. It recounts the experiences of the author and different groups of 'pilgrims' who together spent a week or less in one of the township communities of Gauteng (South Africa) in order to be alongside fellow Christians whom they had not been allowed to visit until 1994. But now, in the post-apartheid era, the township folk can welcome anyone to their homes and offer to them typical, generous African hospitality. Trevor Hudson describes the painful 'awakening' of many of the pilgrims to the horrors that had been happening 'under their very noses' as it were, in those days of oppression and persecution, and about which, through sheer ignorance, they could take no action and feel no pain.

He writes from the particular context of South Africa and in following his suggestion to go on a Pilgrimage of Pain and Hope it would be necessary to adapt to the particular context and culture in which it would take place. But whether or not we follow the particular course of action which Trevor Hudson outlines, there is something in this book for everyone who is serious about the inner journey to wholeness, compassion and more ardent discipleship; who seeks to be more aware, more present to others and less compulsively caring. There is real wisdom here which can be absorbed and applied individually as well as corporately – for we all need to go on pilgrimage.

It is an eminently readable book, deeply personal (i.e. touching the heart as well as the mind), and frequently very searching. Its authenticity stems from the lived experiences on which he draws – his own or that of other pilgrims – to illustrate the venture he encourages us so persuasively to try in our own congregations. It is also a highly practical book, suggesting tests to be carried out personally, discussion points for groups and plans, programmes and practical tests to launch out on a Pilgimage of Pain and Hope.

If there is one thing that stands out from all others, for me, in this book, it is his oft-repeated emphasis on the need for *reflection on our experiences* – which, indeed, is the title of one of his chapters. Who was it who said, 'the unexamined life is not worth living'? Certainly Trevor Hudson reinforces that statement and presses home the need to reflect on our encounters, circumstances, inner thoughts and feelings, reactions etc. For such in-depth reflection, one must spend time in solitude and silence, and the insistence upon the importance of carving out solitude time is made gently but powerfully.

Some may be tempted to think that it's all right for Trevor Hudson. As a pastor he has plenty of time to pray and reflect. But I happen to know that he is one of the busiest and most sought-after ministers in South Africa – as a preacher, retreat-giver and counsellor. *And* he gives high priority to family time. Yet, I know too, that he faithfully guards his times of solitude and silence, regarding them as absolutely crucial to his ministry. Without them, he would be in danger of missing the Divine Whisper and of acting out of his own compassion rather than God's.

I don't imagine anyone could read this book without feeling challenged and enriched in some way – and very humbled by all that he shares with us of the graces of forgiveness and hospitality his pilgrim groups experienced in their encounters with those members of the body of Christ who suffered so grievously, and whose humanity was so appallingly abused, in the past – and yet, somehow, remain unembittered. It made me weep – even though I live in South Africa and know the scene. Perhaps that in itself says something about the power that lies hidden in the book.

Margaret Magdalen CMSV

Foreword

When I write a Foreword to a book, I normally read the manuscript through just once and, after reflection, type up the promised piece. Trevor Hudson's manuscript, however, made such an impact on me that I read it *three times* before I could even begin to find words that I felt might do justice to the text and encourage would-be readers to buy the book, read it, meditate on it and live it. Each of the three times, I read the manuscript avidly – unable to put it down.

I 'happened' to be participating in the annual conference of the Association of Christian Counsellors when I was absorbing the contents of the manuscript for the third time. I wanted each of these fine, caring counsellors to have their own copy of this potentially life-changing book. The following week, I 'happened' to be talking to two members of the Lydia Fellowship – women who have committed themselves to the costly ministry of intercessory prayer. We spoke of the Reconciliation Walks that have been so greatly used by God in recent years. Again, I found myself longing to be able to put this book into the hands of such intercessors as well as every person preparing to set out on a Reconciliation Walk. Within a few days, my husband and I left England for one of our own 'missionary journeys' – a journey that would give us the privilege of leading retreats for missionaries working in some twenty countries. I wished that the book was already in print and that we could put a copy in the hands of each of the missionaries we met.

On our trip, as we watched the news on television, the

plight of the Kurds hit the headlines and it occurred to me that every praying person, whether or not he or she is a professional carer or signed-up pray-er, could be changed by this book: changed by becoming more Christ-like; becoming more Christ-like by catching the Lord's compassion for the hurting, the broken, the marginalised, the forgotten people of our needy world.

I was first inspired by Trevor Hudson's insights when every part of me thrilled to his first book, *Christ-following.* In that book, Trevor mentioned, almost in passing, the retreats with a difference that he had been prompted to lead for members of the church he pastors in South Africa. I was so intrigued by these retreats – or pilgrimages, as he calls them – that I wrote to him asking for more information. The enriching pen-friendship that resulted from this initial contact persuaded me that Trevor was the person to conclude this *Exploring Prayer Series* with much-needed guidance on how our spirituality can express itself in a deeper engagement with a broken world that leaves so many people in pain. That conviction was confirmed when, reading the manuscript for the first time, comments like these leapt out at me:

'Our times cry out for a gospel-shaped spirituality that is both intensely personal and deeply aware of our suffering neighbour.'

'The crucified and risen Christ frequently meets us in the lives of those who suffer.'

'The gospel invites us to apprentice ourselves to Jesus . . .'

The book begins with an explanation of how God gave Trevor the vision for these particular pilgrimages:

' "Take members of your congregation with you to where their

brothers and sisters are suffering", were the simple words that typed themselves across the screen of my mind.'

It goes on to show how we can most effectively 'tip-toe on the holy ground of other people's suffering', and what the Holy Spirit does in *us* when we tread on such hallowed ground. In a unique and powerful chapter, the author opens our eyes to the need for and power of reflecting on any encounter we have with hurting people. Memorably, he claims that: *'we do not learn from experience, we learn from reflecting on experience'* (emphasis mine).

He also provides us with a challenging authenticity test:

'Compassion lies at the heart of the authentic Christ-following life. Any spiritual experience – whether it be one of solitude and silence, prayer and fasting or worship and celebration – which does not result in a deeper concern for our suffering neighbour can hardly be called Christian.'

Before encouraging us to become the kind of Christians in whom 'communion and compassion co-exist', that is, the kind of Christians whose prayer and worship and fellowship overflow into expressed care for those in need, he warns against the very real danger of compassion-fatigue and gives wise and timely guidelines that, if heeded, should ensure that carers learn to live balanced lives.

Each chapter ends with a series of questions that may be used by individuals to aid their own reflection. The same questions have been designed also for use by groups who meet to discuss and share their reactions to and reflections on the book's contents.

While writing this Foreword, another of the author's claims has been ringing in my ears: *'God meets us especially in our interactions with those who suffer.'*

Into my mind has also popped the faces of Christian friends who are social workers, probation officers, Samaritans, members of prayer ministry teams, hospital visitors, Aid workers, people caring for sick relatives and ailing members of their community. I want each of them to have a copy of this healing book. To would-be readers, all I can say in conclusion is, 'buy it for yourself. Buy some for your friends. Its message has the potential to transform you and them.'

Joyce Huggett

Chapter 1

INTRODUCING THE PILGRIMAGE EXPERIENCE

I remember the exact moment the idea of a Pilgrimage of Pain and Hope was born. It was a Sunday afternoon in the bitterly cold August of 1982, and I was driving back home from visiting Soweto with three overseas friends. Together we had attended a small meeting where Jean Vanier, founder of the extraordinary L'Arche movement, had met with a few handicapped people and their families. For almost three hours I had listened quietly to the life stories of ordinary men and women living amidst crushing deprivation and oppression. As I steered my Datsun along the busy highway linking Soweto with neighbouring Johannesburg, their words and faces kept crossing my mind. Then suddenly a thought came into my mind, surprising me with its forcefulness and clarity.

'Take members of your congregation with you to where their brothers and sisters are suffering', were the simple words that typed themselves across the screen of my mind. At that time I was pastoring a largely middle-class suburban congregation safely shielded from the traumatised apartheid context of the early eighties in South Africa. Forced removals, poverty and homelessness were abstractions in the experience of my congregation, as they were in my own. Most of us had never consciously related our Christ-following to these social realities, nor ever had the experience of sharing life with and learning from those who knew firsthand the pain of these social contexts. Perhaps exposing ourselves intentionally to the suffering of others would change us and help us respond in appropriate ways.

I began to pray and plan. Ever since my own beginnings as a disciple of Jesus, I had been struck by the fact that many of the most Christlike spiritual leaders were men and women who lived in close relationship with those who suffered. People like Dorothy Day, Jean Vanier, Henri Nouwen, Cicely Saunders, Jackie Pullinger, Desmond Tutu, were all pilgrims whose words and witness had greatly shaped my understanding of the Christ-following life. Running through all these lives was the common thread of their connection with the poor, the hurting, the broken and the marginalised. Could this be one reason why, I wondered, the transformative grace and caring compassion of Christ seemed so evident in their lives? And could it be that, if we were to spend time with those who were suffering, we would also experience a similar conversion of our hearts and lives?

With questions like these percolating around in my mind, the idea of a Pilgrimage of Pain and Hope gradually began to take form. I contacted friends and colleagues ministering in places where we would want to go, and raised with them the possibility of a small group coming to spend time with them. In response, they shared honestly their concerns and suggestions. We were to come as pilgrims, not as tourists; as learners, not as teachers; as receivers, not as givers; as listeners, not as talkers. Aware that much preparation would be needed to foster an appropriate pilgrim attitude amongst us, I sounded the call for our first pilgrimage experience and waited. Fourteen members of our congregation indicated an interest in the possibility of becoming pilgrims. The adventure had begun.

Eight months later, after much careful preparation and planning, the first Pilgrimage of Pain and Hope was launched. Fifteen pilgrims, ranging in age from seventeen to mid-thirties, left the Kempton Park Methodist Church for an eight-day immersion into the struggles and joys of our suffering neighbours. I doubt whether any of us realised the extent to which our journey together would impact our lives. Suffice to say that, upon returning home, I made a threefold resolve: one, I would plan annually for our congregation a week-long Pilgrimage of Pain and Hope; two, as best as I could in the light of the Christian tradition, I would keep trying to shape the pilgrimage experience into an effective means for spiritual formation; and three, at a very personal level I would seek to become a pilgrim in daily life. On the following pages I share insights and learnings that have become clearer as I have walked along the pilgrimage road. As I do this, I pray that the Spirit will call other Christ-followers to embrace the pilgrimage experience.

Essential Pilgrimage Ingredients

For almost a decade, the Pilgrimage of Pain and Hope was an integral part of our congregation's life. More than one hundred young and not so young adults participated. It became for many of these folk an instrument of lasting personal transformation that led to profound changes in outlook and lifestyle. Repeatedly one could discern, in the lives of the pilgrims, clear evidence of ever-deepening commitment to the Way of Christ. As our pilgrimage experience developed over the years, and we began sharing the ideas with other congregations, it became clear that the concept rested upon three essential ingredients: *Encounter – Reflection – Transformation*. While these will each be more fully explored in later chapters, particularly with regard to their biblical basis and practical implementation in other situations, I want to introduce them briefly now.

First, the Pilgrimage of Pain and Hope is a personal encounter with the pain of our shattered and fragmented societies. Within the South African pilgrimage experience we spent time in a number of different suffering contexts. These ranged from informal housing settlements in desperately impoverished areas, shelters for the homeless and homes for the mentally handicapped, to rehabilitation centres where young people were struggling to break free of their addictions to drugs and alcohol. We found it helpful not to plan more than one exposure every few days. In this way we could actually live with those we were visiting, put names to faces and really talk with our hosts. Encounters were chosen that would specifically challenge any superficial response in possible gospel ministry.

Alongside this encounter with pain, the pilgrimage experience is also an encounter with hope. Scattered throughout these deprived communities are those who resiliently refuse to become prisoners of helplessness and despair. Often unsung and anonymous, these hidden saints shed rays of faith, hope and love upon all whose lives they touch. Moreover, mingled amongst those that suffer and hurt, there are often small bands of ministering Christ-followers seeking to respond and act in faithful and obedient ways. Encountering these signs of hope challenges the pilgrims to examine their own faith responses within their own lives and communities. They see that there is hope in the future, and that their lives can also make a creative difference in a land torn apart by division and suffering. Things do not have to stay as they are. As a church poster once proclaimed, 'Christ has taken the inevitability out of history'.

Secondly, reflection on experience constitutes the next ingredient in the pilgrimage process. Daily, the pilgrims experience a wide range of emotions, circumstances and people. Without reflection they run the risk of losing those insights that can transform us. Hence, throughout the pilgrimage, the participants are given the necessary space to reflect upon what is happening within and around them. Integral to this reflection process is their daily meditation upon the Scriptures in the light of the pilgrimage encounters. Writing out these reflections enables the pilgrims to express their feelings, clarify the issues with which they are wrestling and articulate their desires for future actions of kingdom obedience.

While we can plan into the pilgrimage experience the elements of encounter and reflection, we cannot ensure the third ingredient of transformation. Transformation into greater Christlikeness is always a gift that happens in those generously open to the Holy Spirit. When there is this openness amongst the pilgrims, we have seen that the Spirit deeply transforms human lives. Hearts of stone become hearts of flesh. Reflecting upon this evidence of changed hearts and lives amongst the pilgrims, I have written elsewhere,

The implanted seed of divine compassion begins to flower. Non-sentimental and caring deeds are birthed. Courage is given to speak truth to those principalities and powers intent on destroying the lives of people. Our hearts begin yearning for a society where there is justice and compassion for all. That this can begin to happen in our lives is the testimony of our pilgrims.[1]

Pilgrims in Daily Life

Not every Christ-follower can go away on an eight-day pilgrimage. This became clear as the pilgrims returned home and shared their stories. Many who listened expressed their disappointment that, because of their family and work responsibilities, they could not participate in this annual event. In thinking this through we began to see that these three essential ingredients, *Encounter – Reflection – Transformation,* represent three critical moments of the authentic Christ-following life. As Jesus' disciples we are called into an on-going engagement with our suffering neighbour, continued reflection upon our lives in the light of Scripture and a never-ending process of growing into Christlikeness. In other words, we needed to find a practical way of making the pilgrimage experience part of our daily lives.

Wrestling with this question of how we could become everyday pilgrims, heralded another crucial discovery. Alongside the usual activities of solitude and silence, prayer and fasting, Bible study and meditation, I began to see the possibilities of the pilgrimage experience as a regular spiritual discipline undergirding our daily walk with God. Thus, from the pulpit and in pastoral conversations, I started sharing the idea of building these three pilgrimage ingredients into our everyday lives in a deliberate, conscious and intentional manner. Many responded positively. Again I was astonished to witness how, when we give ourselves faithfully to this pilgrimage discipline, the Spirit of God transforms us into more compassionate and concerned people. So much so that I have reached the conclusion that, for the Christ-follower seeking earnestly to grow in faithful obedience, learning how to become a pilgrim in daily life needs to be a vital component of his or her discipleship.

I must hasten to add that I do not write these words about everyday pilgrimage as a detached and clinical observer. At the time of writing I have not been in a position to lead an eight-day pilgrimage experience for almost six years. Increasing family commitments, change in local church environment together with a different ministry job description have directed my energy and time in other directions. At first I felt that these changes would separate my spiritual journey from the human cries in my midst. However, as I have forged the three essential pilgrimage components into the overall pattern of my life, I feel that my practice of the pilgrimage experience has been even deepened. Indeed, I have come to see myself as a pilgrim in daily life. As I will discuss later, everyday pilgrims seek to cultivate a particular attitude towards life – an attitude which sees the living Christ present in all things, and especially in our encounters with those who suffer.

Contemporary Relevance

Presently we are witnessing an unprecedented upsurge of spiritual searching. Amidst this widespread interest in spirituality there is need for careful discernment. On the one hand, the contemporary church has been inundated by various spiritualities that are obsessively concerned with inner matters and reflect minimal concern for those who suffer. On the other hand, a spirituality of social struggle and liberation, which sidesteps the biblical imperative for personal conversion and transformation, is frequently endorsed. Such endorsement falls prey to the dangerous illusion that we can build a just and compassionate society while we remain the same. Indeed, our times cry out for a gospel-shaped spirituality that is both intensely personal and deeply aware of our suffering neighbour.

Significantly, this desperate need for a more balanced spirituality coincides with the overall goal of the authentic Christ-following life. This goal involves our gradual inner transformation into greater Christlikeness. As disciples of Jesus we are called to live as he would if he were in our place. Whatever else this may mean, it most certainly involves learning how to become a more caring and compassionate person. Compassionate caring, as Paul's magnificent thirteenth chapter of 1 Corinthians points out, is *the* distinguishing mark of faithful discipleship. Keeping this goal before us holds together creatively the inward–outward dynamic so characteristic of Jesus' life, saves us from falling prey to the latest fad in the spiritual supermarket and catapults our lives into a deeper engagement with the brokenness of our world.

Now, while it is the Spirit who enables us to care the way Jesus did, this inward transformation of our hearts requires disciplined effort and planned co-operation. We seldom become more compassionate without working at it. Compassion usually comes as a grace-soaked gift to those who intentionally, consciously and regularly place themselves before God. As we have noted, one practical way of doing this is building the pilgrimage experience into our lives. Whether we embark upon an annual Pilgrimage of Pain and Hope, or seek deliberately to become a pilgrim in daily life, we discover that the crucified and risen Christ frequently meets us in the lives of those who suffer. Hardly ever does this encounter leave us as we are. For this reason, the relevance of the pilgrimage experience for our contemporary situation cannot be overemphasised.

In closing this introductory chapter, I must make it very clear that I am a beginner when it comes to the life of compassion. Others do not always experience me as a caring person. Often I have been deaf to the human cries around me, blind to those in desperate need and indifferent to those structures that hurt and harm God's people. Sometimes I do not even like those with whom I am bound together in Christ. Occasionally those closest to me have felt unappreciated, unnoticed and unloved. Without any doubt my greatest failings have been failures in loving. Yet in spite of my inadequacies, when it comes to the compassionate life and my limited understanding of what it means to be a concerned Christ-follower in our suffering world, I have been enriched enormously by the pilgrimage experience. It would be highly remiss of me not to share what I have been graciously given by those who suffer deeply.

Invitation to Pilgrimage

(Each chapter will be followed by a set of reflective questions which can be used within a small group setting.)

1. Introduce yourself to the group, sharing one aspect of your life which is going very well at the moment.

2. Describe *one* experience where your life was enriched and challenged by someone who suffered greatly.

3. How do you respond to the concept of a 'Pilgrimage of Pain and Hope'?

4. How would you describe your own present spiritual practice?
    A. Non-existent
    B. Inward but lacking the outward dimension
    C. Outward but lacking the inward dimension
    D. Balanced

5. How do you feel about becoming a pilgrim in daily life?

Chapter 2

PREPARING FOR PILGRIMAGE

As we began planning our first Pilgrimage of Pain and Hope, I contacted several people around the country to check out our intentions. One particular phone call, made to a good friend living and ministering in an impoverished rural settlement, exercised a significant influence upon our preparations. After explaining at some length the purpose of our intended pilgrimage, and telling her a little about those travelling with me, I asked whether she would be prepared to co-ordinate our visit from her end. For a few moments she remained silent, almost as if she were trying to find the right words to say something really important. When she did speak her words communicated both encouragement and challenge.

'I'm sure the community will welcome you warmly, but,' she paused briefly and then added, 'please ensure that you come as pilgrims and not as tourists on a sightseeing tour.'

I thought deeply about what she said. Spoken with firm conviction and wise concern her words underlined boldly the necessity for suitable preparation. We were not about to visit sacred shrines or religious venues of historical interest, but rather tip-toe upon the holy ground of other people's suffering. And while certain physical prepara-tions would be essential – decisions about itinerary, routes, means of travel, arrangements with hosts, finances and the like – cultivating an appropriate pilgrim attitude was clearly our top priority. Given the sensitive nature of the Pilgrimage of Pain and Hope, the very last thing we needed was for the pilgrims to adopt attitudes and behaviours usually associated with tourists. Nor, I must hasten to add, did I have any inclination towards becoming a tour-guide for religious sightseers.

My friend's words apply to our everyday lives as Christ-followers as well. The gospel call invites us to apprentice ourselves to Jesus, become pilgrims along the compassionate Way and journey deeper together into the heart and life of God. In our contemporary setting, however, Christians often look more like bustling tourists than faithful pilgrims patiently engaged upon an eternal pilgrimage into the Divine Love. While countless people today make periodic excursions into the spiritual supermarket, especially if something novel is on offer, very few seem willing to sign up as pilgrims in the lifelong adventure of discipleship. Eugene Peterson describes perceptively the situation in which we find ourselves:

> Religion in our time has been captured by the tourist mindset. Religion is understood as a visit to an attractive site to be made when we have adequate leisure. For some it is a weekly jaunt to church. For others, occasional visits to special services. Some, with a bent for religious entertainment and sacred diversion, plan their lives around special events like retreats, rallies and conferences. We go to see a new personality, to hear a new truth, to get a new experience and so, somehow, expand our otherwise humdrum lives.[1]

How, then, do we go about cultivating a pilgrim attitude? Applicable to every apprentice pilgrim, whether we are embarking upon a planned pilgrimage experience or not, this question deserves careful attention. Otherwise our lives run the risk of becoming characterised by aimless drifting, smug self-concern and bland superficiality. Based upon the biblical witness, insights from mentors and my personal experience with the Pilgrimage of Pain and Hope, I want to outline three interwoven ingredients of a pilgrim posture. Besides describing these essential attributes of the Christ-following pilgrim I will also suggest some practical ways through which we can begin forging them into our everyday lives. These three ingredients are:

- learning to be present
- learning to listen
- learning to notice.

Learning to Be Present

I learnt this word during my first year at primary school, even though it would be many years before I discovered some of its rich meanings. To this day I can still remember sitting in my kindergarten classroom while the teacher took her daily register. As our names were called out, each of us answered 'present'. Even if I was half-asleep, or pre-occupied about with whom I was going to play at break, or daydreaming about the sports match due to take place after school, when my name was read out I would automatically say 'present'. Little did I realise then that I was sometimes very far from being present at all. There had taken place, to use an arresting phrase from the writings of Douglas Steere, an 'interior emigration' of my mind and heart from the living moment.[2]

This interior emigration frequently takes place in all of

our lives. In our distracted, frantic and hurried lifestyles we are often not truly present to those around us. I'm sure that, without too much effort, you can think of a recent encounter when you were not really 'all there' for the other person. It happened again for me as I was writing this chapter. I had just picked up my son from school and he was sharing excitedly some news about a forthcoming soccer match in which he would be playing. My mind, however, was preoccupied with something I had to do that afternoon. Sensing that I was totally absent from the present moment my son suddenly said, 'Dad, tell me what I have just said.' I couldn't. And in that moment I felt again the aching sadness of not being present to those I love most.

One heart-wrenching Gospel encounter takes place when the disciples fail to be present to their Master in his time of deep need. Recall briefly that scene of betrayal and dereliction: it is the night before the crucifixion drama and Jesus retreats with his friends to the Gethsemane garden. Aware of the soon-approaching Calvary ordeal, it is for Jesus a time of intense spiritual preparation, rigorous heart-searching and profound anguish of soul. Before leaving them to pray alone, Jesus asks his companions to keep company with him, to sit near him and to stay awake. Three times they let him down by drowsing off and not being present where they are. One can hardly imagine the pain that there must have been in Jesus' heart when he keeps finding them asleep (see Mk 14:32–42.) Could it be that the crucified and risen Christ, as he meets us in those who suffer today, continues to be in pain because of our failure to be present?

I need, therefore, to the very limit of my vision, to try to describe what it means to be truly present. To begin with, being present involves letting go of our constant preoccupations, immersing ourselves in the here and now and giving ourselves wholeheartedly to whatever is at hand. Involving far more than being merely physically present, important as this is, it's about becoming more aware, alert, awake to the fullness of the immediate moment. If we are with another person, it means engaging him or her with all of our heart, our mind, our soul and our strength. Such wholehearted attention requires, from our side, much patience, time and disciplined effort. Yet it is one of the greatest gifts that we can give to those around us, especially our suffering neighbour. When the Russian spiritual writer Catherine de Hueck Doherty was asked by a priest about the kind of contribution he could make within a hurting and broken world, she answered simply, 'Your presence, Father.'[3]

Pilgrims seek to be truly present where they are. By focussing fully on all that the present moment holds, they indicate their willingness to be influenced, perhaps even transformed, by their everyday and commonplace experiences. Their posture before the mystery of life is one of vulnerable openness, non-possessive engagement, reverent participation and childlike wonder. In these respects their mindset differs vastly from that of tourists who, as they drift from one place of interest to another, seek mainly to get whatever pleasure they can. Given the widespread prevelance of this tourist-mentality towards life throughout the western world, and its infiltration into much current spirituality, developing a pilgrim mentality usually begins with a conscious choice to learn how to be present. 'Dear Lord,' we can ask, 'show me how to open my life more generously to the meaning and mystery of the present moment.'

Should you be keen to develop a more present-minded way of living, you may find it helpful to experiment regularly with an exercise that I first came across in the writings of Metropolitan Antony.[4] The basic steps go as follows: Set aside some time, perhaps five minutes, to do nothing. Simply sit down in your room and say, 'I am seated, I am doing nothing. I will do nothing for the next five minutes.' Having declared your intention for this little space of time, decide firmly that during these five minutes you will not be pulled away by anything. Should you find yourself emigrating mentally into the past or the future, bring yourself back to the here and now with the thought, 'I am here in the presence of God, in my own presence, and in the presence of all the furniture that is around me, just still, moving nowhere.' Over the years I have discovered that doing this exercise regularly builds up the capacity to live more deeply in the present within our everyday lives.

Learning to Listen

Listening is the second essential component of the pilgrim attitude. The reason for this is straightforward. Compassion, as we have already seen, lies at the heart of the spiritual journey. We grow towards Christlikeness only as we become more caring. A non caring Christ-follower is a contradiction in terms. However, it is nearly impossible to show real concern, especially for those in pain, unless we first take time to listen. We can only love those to whom we genuinely listen. For this reason, if we intend to put our lives alongside those who suffer and reflect to them the compassion of Christ, our presence must always be a listening one. This could be why James, one of the first spiritual mentors in the Early Church, encourages his readers to 'be quick to listen, slow to speak' (Jas 1:19).

Sadly, Christians are not well known for their listening.

Some years ago, I had an experience that presses home this observation. Together with my family I was strolling along a Johannesburg street when, suddenly, we were surrounded by a group of enthusiastic Christians. Armed with tracts and Bible they stopped us in our tracks and weighed into us with the facts of the gospel. As they spoke about Jesus, and urged us to accept him into our lives, I tried vainly to get a word in. All I wanted to say was, 'Guys, we're on the same side as you,' but they would not give me a chance. Even though they were physically present with us, they failed to communicate the compassionate heart of the Divine Pilgrim. At no stage did they attempt to find out who and where we were before presenting us with the claims of Christ. In their failure to take seriously James' injunction about listening, their actions contradicted their message about God's grace and love.

We do well not to judge this group of zealous Christians. We all know of moments when our failure to listen well has left others feeling isolated, unaccepted and unloved. Thankfully, listening is something that we can all learn to do better. While a few people seem naturally gifted as listeners, most of us need to develop this vital gateway to compassion. Cultivating a listening life, however, does not occur overnight. Few activities require as much energy, effort and patience. Certainly this has been my experience as I have sought to become a better listener. Frequently I catch myself listening badly, and need to return to the basics. Involving at least three basic steps, good listening enables us to grow in the compassionate Way and so become more faithful pilgrims at heart. I outline them briefly in the hope that you may find them helpful:

First, if we want to learn how to listen we need to stop talking. Obviously we cannot speak and listen at the same time. Failure to grasp this commonsense reality impedes many from making any significant progress in the listening life. For unless we bridle our tongues, stop our constant chatter and check our tendencies to interrupt others when they are speaking, it is almost impossible to truly listen to another. Restricting our speech in these ways does not come easily. Deeply ingrained into the tongue are talkative habits that resist determinedly any kind of change. The fact that this little member of the body seems to possess an automatic life all of its own makes it clear that, if we really desire to be listening pilgrims, we will need to discipline ourselves firmly. Practising the silence of not speaking, in those situations which invite our compassionate presence, begins the listening journey.

Secondly, learning to listen involves giving our total attention to the person speaking. Merely being silent does not ensure that we are really listening – it could mean that we are either dead, fast asleep, day-dreaming or totally preoccupied with our own thoughts and feelings. I'm sure that you have had the experience of talking with someone only to sense, from their vacant eyes and faraway look, that they have not heard a word of what you have been saying. By contrast, true listeners are those who concentrate intently upon what someone is saying, the feelings which accompany the words and the silences in-between them. Such concentration communicates non-verbally their genuine and positive interest in what they are hearing. Morton Kelsey captures this dynamic element of the listening process when he writes succinctly,

> Real listening is being silent with another person or group of persons in an active way.[5]

Thirdly, good listeners seek to communicate their understanding of what is being shared with them. In other words, they don't always remain silent. Whenever appropriate they try to clarify what they are hearing the other person say. Of course, like any other communication skill, this reflective listening-style can be badly misused and become a mechanical counterfeit of the real thing. Nonetheless, it is highly unlikely that the person speaking will feel listened to unless we indicate some grasp of what they are wanting to say. I recall how, during my training for pastoral ministry, one of my tutors would constantly say to me, 'Trevor, the most healing gift that you can give to someone in pain is the awareness that you are honestly trying to understand what they are going through, even if you get it wrong.'

Against the background of these basic guidelines I invite you to assess the quality of your present listening ability. Growing in self-awareness as to how we do listen often initiates a fresh commitment to become a better listener. Here are ten straightforward 'yes/no' questions which you can think about. Should you answer positively to any number of them, as I did while putting this quick quiz together, this could be a challenge to develop more consciously a listening heart.

- Am I known as a chatterbox?
- Do I interrupt others in mid-sentence?
- Do I 'switch off' when I disagree with what's being said?
- Do I complete other peoples' sentences?
- Am I often preoccupied during conversations with my own thoughts and feelings?
- Do I plan my answer while others speak?
- Am I afraid of silences in conversations?
- Do I tend to jump in with my own story and take over, instead of listening?

- Am I often impatient while listening?
- Do those closest to me often complain that I don't listen to them?

Learning to Notice

Christ-followers live in the faith that the Divine Presence inter-penetrates all of our lives. Apostle Paul witnesses to this startling reality when, in his message to the Athenians, he declares boldly that God is always near, 'For "In him we live and move and have our being" ' (Acts 17:28). Writing later to the Ephesians he brings this conviction into even sharper focus when he writes that there is '. . . one God and Father of all, who is above all and through all and in all' (Eph 4:6). Whether we acknowledge it or not, the Holy One enfolds each of our lives, pours out continuously the Divine Love upon us and communicates constantly with us. Wherever we may be standing – in the kitchen or the workplace – is holy ground. Jesus said to his disciples in the closing moments of his earthly ministry, 'And remember, I am with you always, to the end of the age' (Mt 28:20).

While God encounters us wherever we are, he meets us especially in our interactions with those who suffer. We learn this from Jesus himself who, as God come in the flesh, identifies himself deeply with suffering men and women. Right from the outset of his public ministry there is an intimate connection with the broken and hurting. He touches the leper, befriends the outcast, delivers the oppressed, welcomes the sinner and forgives the guilty. On the cross he goes one radical step further and identifies himself totally with every sinned-against human being. In his cry, 'My God, my God, why have you forsaken me?' (Mk 15:34), he becomes one with all who feel devastated, abandoned and cut off from God in their suffering. So totally does he connect himself with those in pain that he says to his disciples:

'Truly I tell you, just as you did it to one of the least of these who are members of my family, you did it to me.'
(Mt 25:40)

If God comes so close to us in our everyday experiences and encounters, we must learn how to notice the Divine Presence. Discerning what God is doing and saying in our midst lays the foundations for the faithful pilgrim's responses. I remember learning this from my first 'formal' spiritual director back in 1978. Once a month we would come together to reflect upon my pilgrimage with Christ. Our times together tended to follow a very similar pattern. Usually I began by sharing with her what had taken place in my life over the past few weeks. Besides talking about my experiences of prayer and meditation upon the Scriptures, I would speak also about how things were going at work, my relationships at home and with friends, as well as my involvement with those living in painful situations. After I had finished sharing, my soul-friend would often ask an intriguing question, 'I wonder where God is active in all of this?'

This simple question kept reminding me of the biblical truth that God could be encountered everywhere and in anything. Looking back to the beginnings of my walk with Christ, I realise that I lived in a state of inner segregation. Somehow I tended to separate my life into two distinct compartments – the spiritual and the non-spiritual. Into the former I placed activities like going to church, attending fellowship groups, reading the Bible and witnessing; while the latter comprised the rest of my life's activities.

Not surprisingly this division led to tragic splits in my spiritual journey between the sacred and the secular, the material and the spiritual, the visible and the invisible, and eventually between God and most of my life. Perhaps sensing this, my spiritual director was gently fostering a new attitude within me, an attitude that would learn how to notice the reality and experience of God in all things.

But my spiritual director did more than merely raise a question about the whereabouts of God's presence. In our conversations she would encourage me to be attentive to my inner responses regarding whatever I was living through. By helping me to express these thoughts and feelings, and to reflect on them, she was slowly teaching me how to discern the Divine Whisper. For while God speaks in a variety of ways – through creation, interactions with others, the preaching and teaching of the church, in the cry of our suffering neighbour and, most importantly, in our meditations upon Scripture – the inward effect of being addressed usually takes the shape of a distinctive thought or feeling that we may have. These movements of heart and mind are the way God speaks to us; they are the silent sounds of God's small, still voice. Noticing them draws us deeper into God's heart, sensitises our hearts to the promptings of the Spirit and guides our steps along the pilgrimage road.

This is precisely what happens for the two heartbroken Emmaus pilgrims returning home from Jerusalem after the crucifixion. As they trudge along the road after the fateful events of that first Good Friday they are joined by Jesus in a form that they do not immediately recognise. When he asks them what they are talking about, their story flows out. They share with him how their leader, whom they had hoped would liberate Israel, was handed over to be sentenced to death and was crucified. Moreover, three days later some women had gone to his tomb only to find it empty. At first Jesus listens attentively and then, almost rudely, interrupts the two travellers and begins to explain from the Scriptures how the Messiah had to suffer. As he speaks, his words affect the pilgrims inwardly. Later, their reflections upon these inner responses confirm the identity of the stranger as the risen Jesus. They say to one another, 'Were not our *hearts* burning within us while he was talking to us on the road . . .?' (Lk 24:32, my italics).

How do we nurture this pilgrim mentality of noticing what God is doing and saying within our lives? Allow me to describe a simple exercise that helps us to begin: take a sheet of paper, or a journal if you use one, and list randomly the experiences and encounters of the last twenty-four hours. Next to each item jot down how you thought and felt about them. Reflect prayerfully upon these affective responses, these inner movements of heart and mind, asking the Spirit of God to draw your attention to the Divine Whisper. Certain key questions may facilitate this discernment process:

- Which draw me in the direction of a fuller and more creative life?
- How am I being invited into a closer walk with God; a greater openness towards others; a deeper regard for myself.
- In what ways am I being attracted towards a life more expressive of the compassionate Spirit of Jesus?

Amidst the numerous responses and reactions that jostle around inside our lives, these three questions assist us to notice those gentle inner nudges through which God may be seeking to lead us into greater fullness of life.[6]

To this day I remain thankful for those words spoken by

my friend before our first Pilgrimage of Pain and Hope. They remind us that, if we ever choose to enter the world of another person's suffering, we must cultivate a genuine pilgrim attitude. Hopefully the reasons are now clear. Being present roots the relationship with our hurting neighbour in the reality of the here and now moment. Listening to his or her human cry communicates our presence as a caring and compassionate one. Noticing the Divine Presence at the heart of their suffering opens our inner eyes and ears to what God may be doing and saying. Should we therefore decide to embrace the pilgrimage experience, and build its ingredients into our everyday lives, this never-ceasing preparation of the heart constitutes the most important way in which we can prepare ourselves.

Invitation to Pilgrimage

1. Under the headings 'tourist' and 'pilgrim' draw two columns on a sheet of paper. Brainstorm your immediate responses to these two words. Compare the two lists and notice their similarities and differences.

2. How do you sometimes experience an 'interior emigration' from the present moment?

3. Share your response to the quick quiz (pp 37–38) on your listening style.

4. Share *one* way in which you experience the Divine Presence in your everyday life.

5. In what *one* way do you desire to cultivate a genuine pilgrim attitude towards life?

Chapter 3

ENCOUNTERING OUR
SUFFERING NEIGHBOUR

For over twenty-five years I have pursued the call of being a pastor. This daily work includes the daunting responsibility of enabling others to grow as disciples of Jesus. In responding to this vocational challenge I lead Bible studies, host silent retreats, offer spiritual counsel, conduct teaching seminars, participate in small groups and engage in countless pastoral conversations. While all these ministry endeavours are definitely worthwhile, without the specific ingredients which the pilgrimage experience offers, these efforts at spiritual formation lack something vital. Arising from careful observation of the changed lives of those pilgrims who have opened themselves to their suffering neighbours, this conviction shapes significantly the way in which I now encourage others along the Christ-following path.

I encourage the pilgrimage experience as a method for personal transformation and change not only because of what I see in the lives of others. In my personal experience, my suffering neighbour is where I meet the crucified and risen Christ. Each day I am given privileged access into the lives of those who suffer greatly. These daily encounters with the terminally ill, the depressed, the economically poor, the retrenched, the divorced, the childless, the addicted, the forgotten elderly, the bereaved, and other suffering men and women, affect profoundly my under-standing and experience of the Christ-following life. These relationships have been one of the most significant means used by the Spirit in my on-going conversion.

It comes as little surprise to learn that great spiritual directors often encourage first-hand encounter with bro-ken and hurting people. One case study that springs immediately to mind was the relationship between Baron Friedrich von Hugel and Evelyn Underhill. Evelyn grew up in a comfortable London home, married a successful lawyer and gave her life to a study of the Church's great mystics. During her middle forties, in the midst of a deep mid-life despair, she approached the German Christian and asked him to be her spiritual guide. Through his coun-sel, given mainly in the form of written letters, he enabled her to discover a richer and more personal relationship with Jesus. Significantly, he suggested that, in order for her faith to descend from her head into her heart, she should have regular contact with the poor. In one letter he writes,

I believe you ought to get yourself, gently and gradu-ally, interested in the poor; that you should visit them, very quietly and unostentatiously, with as little incor-poration as possible into Visiting Societies etc. You badly want de-intellectualising or at least developing homely human sense and spirit dispositions . . . I would carefully give preference to the two weekly visitations of the poor above anything else, excepting definite home and family duties . . .[1]

Unless we try to describe what happens in these exposure moments, our discussion about the value of the pilgrim-age experience remains at the abstract level. Indeed, some feel that this structured form of contact lacks the spontaneity characteristic of heartfelt compassion and therefore has its limitations. Combining insights gleaned from the Scriptures, wisdom gained from influential mentors and lessons learnt on the pilgrimages themselves, I believe that when we open our lives to those who suffer, three things happen: the Spirit of God

- opens blind eyes
- uncovers inner poverty
- reveals hidden riches.

Such awareness and self-knowledge constitute crucial pre-requisites for travelling down the conversion road. Allow me to elaborate briefly.

Opening Blind Eyes

Have you ever been struck by the emphasis that Jesus gives to our eyesight? Not only does he frequently heal people of physical blindness, he also invites his hearers to evaluate the quality of their vision (see passages like Mt 6:22; 7:3; Mk 8:23; Jn 4:35). He believes strongly that the way we see others determines our behaviour towards them. This appears to be the central thrust of his provocative parable about the Last Judgment, in which the Judge separates people from one another like sheep from goats. Those on the right are pronounced 'blessed', while those on the left are sent away to fend for themselves. Notice that the criterion upon which the judgment takes place has to do with how much or how little each group had seen. In his comment upon this Gospel passage John Claypool observes:

Those on the right obviously had learned to utilize all

their capacities of sight – the eyes of the body, of the mind, of the heart. And because of their complete sight, those people had been moved to respond to the sick, the hungry, the naked, the imprisoned, the outcast. They had seen beneath surface appearances to the Ultimate dimensions – where all persons are in God and God is in all persons.[2]

It's easy today not to recognise these sacred depths in our suffering neighbour. The reasons for this blindness of heart vary. On the one hand, constant media bombardment of human need often breeds a bland familiarity that generalises suffering men and women into groups like 'the poor', 'the homeless', 'the unemployed', 'the elderly'. Within these generalisations we lose sight of the spiritual dimensions present in each human being. On the other hand, our anonymous encounters with beggars, street children, destitute men and women, give rise to a sense of powerlessness that causes many of us to look away in another direction. Just yesterday I experienced this when I stopped at a traffic light. Standing on the corner was a young mother, a crying baby strapped to her back, holding a card that asked for food or work. Almost automatically I avoided her eyes. I did not want even to acknowledge her presence, let alone see Christ in her.

Of course we cannot meet all the needs around us. Nonetheless, tragic consequences flow from this failure to recognise our suffering neighbour for who he or she really is. These range from a cold indifference to the human cries around us, to cynicism and even resentment towards people's needs; a lack of engagement with those 'principalities and powers' that crush and oppress – to a tragic loss of our own humanness. However – and this is one of the aims of the pilgrimage experience – when we share personally with some of those who suffer, put names to faces, listen to their life-stories, receive the gifts they have to offer, we create a climate in which we learn to see differently. These personal encounters help the pilgrims to see their suffering neighbour as a brother or sister, made in the image of God and in whom Christ dwells. Such recognition and awareness generates a new way of relating that makes genuine compassion possible.

Perhaps now we can understand better the conversation between a wise old spiritual master and his disciples. Once he asked them, 'How can we know when the darkness is leaving and the dawn is coming?'

The disciples were quiet for a moment and then one answered, 'When we can see a tree in the distance and know that it is an elm and not a juniper.' Another responded, 'When we can see an animal, and know that it is a fox and not a wolf.'

'No,' said the old man, 'those things will not help us.'

Puzzled, the students asked, 'How then can we know?'

The master leaned over and said to them quietly, 'We know the darkness is leaving and the dawn is coming when we can see another person and know that this is our brother or our sister; for otherwise, no matter what time it is, it is still dark.'[3]

You may find it helpful to reflect upon the health of your own current eyesight. Several questions could prove useful in this diagnostic exercise. They include the following :

- Is my seeing limited by the other person's colour, class or culture?
- Do I focus upon outward appearances in my dealings with people?
- Do I see people primarily as groups?
- Do I view others using my first impressions, rather

than hearing them out?

- Do I look at possessions as being more important than persons?

Should you answer affirmatively to one or more of these questions, I invite you to pray a one-sentence prayer that I use often in my own personal devotions, 'Lord Jesus, please help me to see each person whom I meet today as someone of infinite value and immense worth.'

Uncovering Our Inner Poverty

One person whose life-example and writings influence the underlying thinking of the Pilgrimage of Pain and Hope is Jean Vanier. In August 1964, Jean bought a small house in Trosly-Breuil, a small village to the north of Paris, and invited two mentally-handicapped men to share it with him. So began L'Arche (the Ark), an extraordinary movement where people who are often rejected and marginalised in today's success-bound world live together with 'assistants'. In these family-like communities the inhabitants get to know each other, learn how to share joys and struggles, and help one another to live more fully. Today there are L'Arche homes scattered all over the world, demonstrating an alternative way of caring for the handicapped. But their real significance goes deeper. As Jean Vanier was to learn, and as his writings make clear, these encounters with suffering men and women uncover the poverty of our hearts.

Jean began to discover this with his first two family members, Raphael and Philip. Both these men were physically as well as mentally handicapped. Raphael had a vocabulary of about twenty words and a very limited understanding, while Philip could only walk with a crutch. Sharing their lives on a daily basis plunged Jean into a world of indescribable anguish that was to initiate within his own heart a process of profound inner transformation. Hidden inside the hearts of the two men was a deep cry for communion, friendship and love. However, these qualities of heart did not come easily to Jean. All his life he had been brought up to be efficient, to get things done, to intellectualise, to compete. It was not easy for him just to be with people, let alone be with people who could hardly speak or had little to speak about. Movingly Jean describes his painful discovery of the hardness in his own heart,

> I discovered something which I had never confronted before, that there were immense forces of darkness and hatred within my own heart. At particular moments of fatigue or stress, I saw forces of hate rising up inside me, and the capacity to hurt someone who was weak and was provoking me! That, I think, was what caused me the most pain: to discover who I really am, and to realise that maybe I did not want to know who I really was! I did not want to admit all the garbage inside me.[4]

This honesty invites us to reflect thoughtfully on our own lives. Pause for a brief moment and ask yourself whether you have ever experienced similar feelings in your own personal interactions with the hurt and broken. Certainly we did on our Pilgrimages of Pain and Hope. As we encountered the different worlds of suffering around us, and spent time with those living there, many of us were confronted with the garbage in our own hearts. Ranging from feelings of indifference, anger, frustration and superiority, to deeply-rooted prejudices towards others different in colour and culture, we discovered that this inner brokenness often prevented genuine relationship from taking place. It became clear to those involved in the pilgrimage experience that, if we really desired to live the compassionate life, we would need to recognise and engage our own inner poverty.

This is seldom easy. Facing our inner poverty means letting go of virtuous illusions about ourselves as guileless, respectable and caring people. So, rather than acknowledge the garbage in our hearts, we pretend that all is well within. Or we try to escape our own ugliness by losing ourselves in frantic religious activity, doing things for those in need instead of entering into communion and friendship with them. Whatever shape the poverty of our hearts may take, our immediate response is usually to hide or ignore it. Recently I addressed a women's group involved in valuable charity work. During my talk I suggested the importance of confessing the darker and more destructive sides of our personalities. Afterwards one lady came up to the podium and said, 'I don't understand what you are trying to get at. I love everyone that I meet.'

Practically, how do we engage creatively our inner poverty? First and foremost, when our negative feelings and reactions emerge in our dealings with suffering people, we can acknowledge them. We cannot engage what we do not acknowledge. Then we can find a trusted friend, a spiritual companion or a competent counsellor with whom to share these darker aspects of ourselves. Few of us are able to face our darkness inside without the listening and non-judgemental presence of another human being. Once we have acknowledged the aggression and violence and hatred that lurks inside, we can begin to take responsibility for what is there. As Christ-followers this involves affirming our goal to become more like him and expressing those aspects of our lives that lead us in this particular direction. Rarely does God change our hearts without our determined co-operation and disciplined effort. As Paul writes,

> Keep on working with fear and trembling to complete your salvation, because God is always at work in you to make you willing and able to obey his own purpose.
>
> (Phil 2:13, GNB)

Secondly, we engage our inner poverty creatively by calling out for God's help. Our vain attempts at trying to change ourselves remind us that we cannot grow into greater Christlikeness in our own strength. By ourselves we are totally unable to root out the dark forces of our hearts. Besides the support and care of trusted companions willing to bear with us in our wretchedness, we need power from beyond ourselves. Something needs to take place within us that we ourselves cannot do. Realising the impossibility of self-redemption, we cry out to God and ask for what we need. As we do this we discover that God meets us in our place of deepest brokenness, accepts us as we are and offers us with crucified hands the gifts of grace and mercy. And while this prayer encounter seldom expels completely the darkness within our hearts, it enables us to overcome our poverty within and keep moving towards our goal of becoming more compassionate followers of Christ.

On our Pilgrimages of Pain and Hope I adapt a favourite prayer exercise to help the pilgrims experience these two steps. You may like to try this meditation when, in your interactions with suffering men and women, you find yourself confronted with your own inner poverty. Here is the basic outline: Imagine yourself sitting quietly in the room of your heart. Its general state of untidiness and messiness represents your failure in connecting compassionately with the hurt and broken. As you look around at the unmade bed, overflowing refuse bin, the clothing lying around, the unwashed dishes piled high in the sink, you hear an accusing voice say, 'You are useless when it comes to caring for others. Why don't you give up seeking to be a Christ-follower. You will never be an effective instrument of the Divine Love.'

As you listen to these words from the accuser you hear the sound of a gentle, persistent knocking at the door. You get up from your chair, walk across the room and open the door. Standing before you in the doorway is the figure of the crucified and risen Jesus, lantern in hand, the other hand raised to knock, a crown of thorns pressed into his head. He says to you, 'Look at me. I stand at the door. I knock. If you hear me call and open the door, I'll come right in and sit down to supper with you' (Rev 3:20, The Message).

As you open the door wider the ever-present Lord enters your room. The light from his lantern radiates warm rays of hope into the shabbiness around you. Together you sit down at the table upon which there is bread and wine. He asks you to tell him about the dark forces that rise up within you when you are with those who suffer. As you share your heart he listens with acceptance and understanding and empathy. Then he takes a loaf of bread, breaks off a piece and gives it to you with the words, 'This is my body broken for you.' He also takes a cup of wine, blesses it, and shares it with you, saying, 'This is my blood shed for you.' Before he gets up to leave, he places his hand upon your shoulder and says to you by name,

'I will be with you even until the end. Receive now my love to go with you. Bring that love to others, especially to the suffering neighbour that my Father places upon your path. No matter how messy your life may be, I will never give up on you.'[5]

Revealing Our Hidden Riches

Some time ago I spent time meditating on Jesus' well-known words, 'This is my commandment, that you love one another as I have loved you' (Jn 15:12). These words usually leave me feeling very much a failure when it comes to caring for those around me. This time, however, my meditative experience was totally different. As I turned this sentence over in my mind, and thought about its possible meanings for my life, it struck me that Jesus actually believes in my capacity to love as he loves. It seemed as if he was saying to me through these words, 'Trevor, tucked away in your depths there are amazing capacities for loving. Know that you are as capable of loving others as I would if I were in your place. Allow my Spirit to reveal these hidden riches so that you may express them and become the person God wants you to be.'

Further reflection upon Jesus' commandment helped me to understand our lives in a more hopeful and positive way. Not only do we possess considerable inner garbage, but there also lie deep within us enormous God-given resources for compassionate living. I should not have been as surprised as I was. Biblical faith consistently asserts that we have been created by Love, in the image and likeness of Love, that we may learn to love as God does (see passages like Genesis 1:27; Ephesians 5:2; 1 John 4:16). Tragically, this capacity to love gets buried beneath our excessive egoism, our many self-centred choices and our constant preoccupation with our own well-being. In the process we become blind to our hidden riches, unaware of how much we can give to others and consequently fail to become who we are capable of becoming.

Again, one way in which God reveals our hidden riches and helps us towards becoming our true selves, occurs through our encounter with those who suffer. I watch this happening repeatedly in the lives of many pilgrims upon our Pilgrimages of Pain and Hope. As they open themselves to their suffering neighbour, and enter into communion with him or her, their concealed compassionate natures begin to flower. This unfolding of who they truly are finds expression in various ways

- egocentric attitudes and drives start being replaced by responses that are more caring;
- self-centredness slowly gives way to a growing awareness of other people's needs; and,
- in the place of obsessive self-interest, there develops a concern for the common good.

These changes in the lives of the pilgrims show that our interactions with suffering people can reveal, not only what is worst about us, *but also what is most beautiful.*

There are three reasons why our encounters with those who suffer reveal our hidden riches. In the first place, these encounters affect our hearts far more than they do our heads. As pointed out already, we are bombarded constantly with media images and statistics of human misery. Never before have we known so much about the brokenness of our world. However, while we may often discuss and debate what we see on the television or read in the newspapers, these media exposures seldom lead us towards greater compassion. But when the painful realities around us assume a human face to whom we can put a name, and to whose story we can listen, there takes place a meeting of human hearts. Such heart encounters possess the power to uncover the more compassionate dimensions of our natures.

Secondly, whenever we are amongst people in pain – whether it be in a hospice for the dying, a home for the mentally handicapped, a shelter for abused children or a care centre for the elderly – those present call forth the gifts which only our hearts can give. They do not so much need the skills of our hands or the knowledge of our minds, as they do the compassion of our hearts. It is as if the suffering person extends an invitation to us saying, 'Before you do anything for me, please come alongside me. Enter into communion with me so that you can be with me in my pain. Walk alongside me as my friend and companion.' Deep treasures emerge from our hearts when we seek to respond to this cry for friendship, companionship and solidarity.

Thirdly, suffering people evoke the more compassionate sides of our personalities by demonstrating a remarkable capacity to extend themselves in generous caring. One pilgrimage experience stands out vividly in my memory.[6] Some years ago we spent three days sharing the life of a deprived and dispossessed community. Two of the pilgrims, both young women in their early twenties, lived with a family of six in a two-room dwelling. For the duration of their stay the husband and wife insisted that the two pilgrims use their bed while they themselves slept on the floor in the adjoining room with their children. Each morning they found that water had been heated for them over an open fire and a breakfast cooked. When they left they were given a small gift to take with them back to their families.

Our next stay was in an exclusive and affluent suburb of

a major South African city. The same two pilgrims were placed with a couple living alone in a two-storey home. When they arrived, the young adults were asked if they would use their sleeping bags and sleep on the carpet in the family room. Breakfast was cooked for them by the domestic worker, left on the kitchen table, and eaten alone without their hosts. On the last day of their stay you can imagine the shock and surprise for these pilgrims when they discovered upstairs three unused, furnished bedrooms. Their contrasting experience became for all of us on that pilgrimage a powerful demonstration of how our suffering neighbours, through their own compassionate actions, can challenge us to express the hidden riches of our hearts.

In describing how our suffering neighbour can become God's catalyst in our continuing conversion, I do not want to romanticise these encounters. Like ourselves, those who suffer are also sinful, fallible and broken human beings. Nonetheless, when we enter into communion with someone in deep pain and anguish, we do not remain the same. We discover that the relationship has the potential to open our eyes, uncover our inner poverty and reveal our hidden riches. For these reasons, exposing our lives intentionally to our suffering neighbour needs to become a crucial priority in the life of any serious Christ-follower. Otherwise it remains highly doubtful whether we will grow into the compassionate and caring people that God wants us to be.

Invitation to Pilgrimage

1. What has helped you most to grow as a Christ-follower?

2. In the light of the questionnaire on page 47–48 how

would you describe the health of your current eye-sight?

3. Name *one* negative feeling that sometimes surfaces within when you are with a suffering person?

4. How do you respond to your own potential to love as Jesus loved?

5. End your time of group-sharing by sharing together in the imaginative meditation outlined in this chapter (pp 51–52). It may be helpful if someone in the group would prepare this meditation beforehand and then lead the rest of the group through it.

Chapter 4

REFLECTING UPON
OUR EXPERIENCES

One simple sentence, spoken to me by my first pastoral supervisor, exercises a powerful influence upon the way I work as a pastor. His words shape considerably my present understanding of how we can grow in awareness, deepen our spirituality and forge a more compassionate lifestyle. Each week during my initial year of pastoral ministry, as we sat opposite each other in his book-lined study reviewing my daily activities, he underlined the importance of our time together by qualifying a commonly held assumption. 'Always remember, Trevor,' he would say, 'we do not learn from experience, we learn from reflection upon experience.'

Over the years I applied my mentor's counsel both to my own faith-journey and my ministry efforts within the local congregation. As I did so, I became firmly convinced that, unless we value and practise reflection, very little personal transformation occurs. Unreflected-upon experience seldom yields its life-giving secrets. Sadly, too many of us work and live without reflection, without trying to gain any objective perspective on our behaviour, or any understanding of why we do the things we do. Think of how often we make the same mistakes, repeat the same destructive behavioural patterns without ever pausing to look at what may be taking place in our lives. Only when we stop to reflect upon these experiences, and extract their hidden insights, do we open ourselves to the possibilities of real change.

Yesterday, while spending time with a dispirited youth worker, I witnessed again how reflection initiates new beginnings in outlook and behaviour. A spate of difficult pastoral interventions, late night crisis calls, demanding speaking engagements and study assignments had left her lethargic and depleted in energy. When she finished describing her weariness I gave her a clean sheet of paper, asked her to draw two columns with the headings 'Output' and 'Input' and suggested that she list under each the various activities of her past two weeks. There was a complete imbalance. Twenty-five items featured in the first column and only two in the second. Inviting her to reflect upon this variance I asked her how she felt and what she was thinking. For a few moments she was quiet before answering, 'Well, I feel tired when I compare the two lists. Obviously I don't replenish the energy I give out to others. I realise that I cannot keep giving out without taking time to resource myself. Somehow I must develop more balance in my life and find more sources of input. Perhaps God is even speaking to me in my tiredness and weariness about taking better care of myself.'

My young friend's reply illustrates the value of practising reflection. When we carve out the time in our busy schedules to reflect upon what's happening in our inner and outer worlds, those insights necessary for our on-going growth become much clearer. In reflection we can look more closely at our daily activities, observe how we are doing them and try to envisage how they can be done more effectively. Most important of all, a reflective person is more able to discern the Divine Whisper within the emotions, circumstances and events he or she experiences within daily life. As I frequently say to those amongst whom I pastor, 'It's much easier to see where the Spirit of God is leading in our lives when we reflect upon them.'

Examples from both Testaments supply supportive evidence for the value and practice of reflection. On the pages of the Old, Moses' solitary work of sheep-watching provided ample opportunity for him to think over his past experiences. Strikingly, it is against this backdrop that God calls him through the burning bush experience into the twin tasks of people-liberation and nation-building (see Ex 3:1–6). Upon entering the world of the New Testament, we have a model and mentor for the reflective life in Mary. Twice in his Gospel record Luke draws our attention to the way she remembered her past experiences, pondered them in her heart and mulled over their possible meanings (see Lk 2:19, 51). One wonders whether, without their commitment to a life of reflection, these two personalities would have been so wonderfully used by God as they were.

By now it should be clearer why reflection is the second essential ingredient of the pilgrimage experience. As the pilgrims reflect upon their encounters with suffering neighbours, and become more aware of their inner responses, they uncover insights that can change their lives. Moreover, the practice of reflection fine-tunes their antennae to hear God speaking to them through the 'human cries' around them, a kind of listening which often lays the basis for future actions of compassionate ministry and mission. On our pilgrimages we find that three particular activities facilitate the reflective lifestyle. Since they are helpful for pilgrims in daily life, as well as those who embark upon a Pilgrimage of Pain and Hope, I will describe each one. They are:

- keeping a pilgrim journal
- structuring a daily solitude-time
- sharing our experiences with each other.

Keeping a Pilgrim Journal

Each day during the Pilgrimage of Pain and Hope, participants are invited to record their reflections upon what they are experiencing. In their 'pilgrim journals', they write down their responses to both the outward and inward dimensions of the pilgrimage experience, enabling them to gain as much as they can from their privileged encounters with suffering people. Amidst these daily reflections the pilgrims catch glimpses of their hidden hearts, discover insights necessary for their continuing conversion and learn to discern the Divine Whisper. In order to help them notice their responses, the following five questions are suggested to them as an aid to reflection:

- What did we do today?
- What encounter made the deepest impression on me?
- What are my thoughts and feelings about this encounter?
- What actions of hope and obedience did I see?
- What do I sense Christ saying through my day's experiences?

Three important benefits flow out of this discipline of writing down our reflections. First, keeping a pilgrim journal helps us to keep track of our significant experiences and encounters. Our memories are fallible. Many of us can hardly remember clearly what happened last week, let alone recall some of the thoughts and feelings that we had. In contrast, when we write out what takes place in our lives, and record our inner responses, our reflections remain with us forever. Whenever necessary we can return to a particular experience and remember its effect on us, by reading the relevant page of our journal.

Secondly, keeping a pilgrim journal encourages us to persevere in the practice of reflection. Growing in self-knowledge and awareness evokes enormous resistance from within ourselves, especially when we start to discover aspects about ourselves which we would prefer not to know. In these moments the temptation to avoid the inner journey, lose ourselves in compulsive busyness and focus on externals increases in intensity. Disciplining ourselves to find a quiet place to sit down with pen and paper and write out our reflections upon what is taking place in our lives helps us to overcome this temptation and counter the resistant forces. Elizabeth O'Connor, a widely-respected spiritual guide, gives us this piece of wisdom:

> Among our primary tools for growth are *reflection, self-observation* and *self-questioning.* The journal is one of the most helpful vehicles we have for cultivating these great powers in ourselves. We all have these powers but we need structures that encourage us to use and practice them. Journal writing is enforced reflection. When we commit our observations to writing we are taking what is inside us and placing it outside us. We are holding a piece of our life in our hands where we can look at it, and meditate on it, and deepen our understanding of it.[1]

Thirdly, keeping a pilgrim journal helps us to listen to God. Recall the point made earlier, in Chapter 2, about how the Divine Whisper usually takes the shape of a distinctive thought or feeling. If this be true, writing out our affective responses to life aids us greatly in discerning the still, small voice. While not everything that surfaces into our consciousness comes from God, putting down these movements of heart and mind on paper makes them concrete and enables us to sift through them more thoroughly. Using the three questions outlined on page 33 we can then reflect upon our thoughts and feelings, and ask the Holy Spirit to draw our attention to the Divine Whisper. Reflection practised regularly along these lines leads us not only into greater self-understanding, but it also deepens our dialogue and communion with God.

I can personally vouch for the value of writing down our reflections. About four or five times each week I sit down in a quiet place, with Bible, journal and pen. After spending some time meditating upon a passage from Scripture, I jot down whatever comes to mind. Sometimes these thoughts and feelings relate directly to what I have just read; at other times they suggest practical tasks that need attention; people to see, or things to do in my family relationships. Often they emerge from past significant people-encounters, especially with those who suffer. Once I have finished writing, I then re-read what is before me and ask the Holy Spirit to help me discern the Divine Whisper. As the following excerpt from a recent journal entry shows, these written meditations deepen my knowledge about myself, enable me to hear what God may be saying and show me the way to go forward.

'Spent time yesterday with Gill in hospital. Presently she is suffering terribly from the horrendous effects of her chemotherapy treatment. I was deeply moved by our time together, and found myself struck by her remarkable courage. When I mentioned this she answered quietly, "God gives this courage to all of us. We only need to use it." Her words echo within me as I sit here in the quiet.

They remind me that there are buried assets in all of our lives, including my own. Lord Jesus, make me aware of those positive traits that lie dormant in my personality. Help me today to recognise in particular my capacity for courageous living and to develop it to your glory and for your sake.'

Structuring a Daily Solitude-Time

While we can practise reflection in the midst of activity and busyness, the truly reflective life requires time alone. Hence, on the Pilgrimage of Pain and Hope we programme thirty minutes of solitude time into each day. During this time the pilgrims retreat to reflect on their encounters with suffering people, meditate on selected Bible passages, write in their journals and pray. Without these solitary moments it is unlikely that they would do the reflective work so necessary for personal transformation and change. So closely are solitude and reflection connected that it is hard to imagine the one without the other.

In teasing out the threads that link solitude with the reflective lifestyle, several closely-related thoughts come to mind. To begin with, the experience of being alone creates the space in which we can gather ourselves together, relax and become quieter within. It's nearly impossible to reflect deeply, either upon our lives or a Bible passage, when our bodies and minds are not at peace. By contrast, when we draw aside to some quiet place, we provide our souls with a proper environment in which to become still. Such stillness enables us to be in touch with our feelings and thoughts. We can better respond to whatever is taking place in our lives, and become more sensitive to the Divine Whisper. No wonder we are advised in the Psalms, 'Be still and know that I am God' (Ps 46:10).

Another thought about this connection between solitude and reflection has to do with stopping in order to see more clearly. Sometime ago we took a train trip as a family from Johannesburg to Cape Town. Early in the morning, as the train raced along, we looked out of the windows at the passing landscape. Travelling at such great speed, it was difficult to register anything fully. Only when we stopped at the small stations, were we able to fully take in the surrounding countryside. In similar vein, our everyday lives become blurred when we are constantly on the go. Solitude time, however, halts our rushing flow of experience so that we can gain clearer insight into what is churning around within and about us. In the well-known words of the sign at a railroad crossing, being alone enables us to STOP – LOOK – LISTEN.

Lastly, solitude provides that quality of detachment which all true reflection requires.[2] Unless we separate ourselves in some way from our ordinary round of activities, and unhook ourselves from their clutches, it is nearly impossible to enter the reflective process. Moreover we become like ping pong balls that bounce back and forth with every emotion and outward encounter, caught up in habitual ways of thinking and doing things. In strong contrast, taking time out to be alone gives us the critical distance to step back from what we are experiencing and think more objectively about it. After such solitude-time, and the reflection which goes with it, we are able to re-enter our world and respond more consciously and maturely to the challenges that confront us.

Detaching ourselves from our everyday involvements for brief time periods helps enormously when we battle with strong emotions. Again, the pilgrimage experience has been the laboratory for my learning in this regard. As the pilgrims encounter suffering, and become increasingly aware of the human cries in their midst, difficult feelings often begin to surface in their lives. These can range from a paralysing sense of powerlessness and inadequacy to deep distress; or from fear and guilt to a cold indifference. Those who honestly write out their feelings, and reflect upon them in solitude, respond more constructively than those who avoid this inner work. Meaningful actions of ministry and mission, it would appear, are usually born out of a mature detachment penetrated by reflection and prayer.

In my own everyday pilgrimage I find three kinds of solitude-time necessary. Each day I enjoy taking 'little solitudes', to use Catherine de Hueck Doherty's expressive phrase, in which to savour some time alone.[3] This may involve turning off the car radio as I commute, or taking a five-minute break between counselling sessions, or going for an evening stroll. During these quiet interludes I remind myself of God's companionship, meditate upon what's happening in my life and listen for any gentle urgings that may be given about upcoming tasks. Also, before my working day begins I set aside some time, lasting anywhere between twenty and forty minutes, for conversation with God built around the Scriptures. And then, once a year, I go away for a forty-eight hour silent retreat where no phone or fax can interrupt. This yearly spiritual checkup allows for an in-depth look at my life, a re-ordering of priorities and some goal-setting for the future. I shudder to think of where my life would be without the reflection that these solitude-times facilitate.

Sharing Our Experiences

The Pilgrimage of Pain and Hope is a journey shared with others. We travel together in cars. We share each day in least one common meal. We meet for daily worship and discussion. We spend time playing as a group and, even when we separate to sleep over with our various hosts, we do so in pairs. During our time together deep bonds of friendship and belonging build up, providing a warm environment for mutual encouragement, care and celebration. Even when conflicts and disagreements arise, as they often do, these are worked through in community. By the end of the pilgrimage the pilgrims have usually tasted in some small but significant way what genuine fellowship is all about.

In all the ways described above, the pilgrimage experience embodies within its own communal life the corporate dimensions of the authentic Christ-following life. When we turn towards the crucified and risen Christ, and open our hearts to receive him, he enters them with his arms around his sisters and brothers. We cannot say, 'Lord Jesus, I want to be with you, but not with your family.' Genuine repentance and faith nearly always immerse the disciple in a common life. We follow Jesus bonded together with others who also have been called. Within this family-belonging our growth in discipleship takes place. To be in Christ, and to progress towards maturity, requires community. Kenneth Leech holds together in creative tension the personal and corporate aspects of the life of faith when he writes,

> Being a Christian, in the New Testament understanding, is thus not a purely personal, but a social reality. At the same time, within the body of Christ, there is an encounter with God, and a continuing and developing relationship with God, at the personal level.[4]

It follows that the practice of reflection, in order to be truly biblical, needs also to be done with others. For this reason each Pilgrimage of Pain and Hope has a time reserved for the sharing of personal experiences. Usually this life-sharing forms part of the liturgy for our daily worship. As we sit around in a circle, each pilgrim is invited to share whatever he or she would like arising from their personal reflections in the solitude. On the first day of the pilgrimage the guidelines for this sharing process are discussed, clarified and agreed upon. Since they have proven themselves immensely helpful, and can be adapted for any group experience within the church, I outline them briefly as follows:

- Everything shared within the group is strictly confidential;
- While every person is invited to share, no one is compelled to do so;
- When sharing, it is important to focus upon one's personal thoughts and feelings;
- When listening it is important not to interrupt, or try to 'fix up' the person speaking;
- After a person has spoken there will be a brief silence to reflect on what has been said;
- Attendance is essential to our life together as a community;
- The facilitator may step in if the process goes astray, or make comments when everyone has finished sharing.

Many pilgrims find this group experience beneficial. In the process of articulating their personal thoughts and feelings, and listening to those of others, they discover that their reflections expand and deepen. As they take turns to share, new insights emerge that open their eyes to what they had not seen before. Also, the activity of listening attentively to how another person perceives a certain reality or experience broadens their own individual way of seeing. Like all of us with our own biases and prejudices, the pilgrims are all vulnerable to the dangers of tunnel-vision, and so need to give careful attention to the perceptions of others. Since God often shows one part of the picture to one person, and another part to another person, this kind of mutual sharing goes a long way towards discerning what God may be saying through the various pilgrimage encounters.

I hope this chapter has encouraged you to develop a more reflective lifestyle. If it has, you may want to experiment with the following exercise. For a period of one week, why not commit yourself to a daily solitude time in which you can unplug yourself from your usual activities. In this quiet place yield yourself to God and ask for the gifts of divine wisdom and discernment. Record in a notebook your activities during the preceding twenty-four hours. Make notes of the people you encountered, the things you learnt, your feelings and the impressions you sense God wanted you to have. Remind yourself that God often speaks through our feelings and thoughts. Therefore, when you complete your daily journal entry, re-read what you have written and ask the Holy Spirit to deepen your sensitivity to the Divine Whisper. At the end of the week evaluate your attempts at reflection and see whether they have made you more aware of God's presence in your everyday life. If they have, you may decide to practise reflection in this particular way on a regular basis. Whatever your decision, keep close to your heart Paulo Friere's admonition that unless we become reflective people we will never be among those 'who will carry out radical transformations'.[5]

Invitation to Pilgrimage

1. 'We do not learn from experience, we learn from reflection upon experience.' How do you respond to this statement?

2. How do you respond to the challenge of keeping 'a pilgrim journal'?

3. What place does solitude have in your present way of life?

4. In what ways do you share your spiritual journey with others?

5. If you experimented with the suggested exercise over the past week, share your experience with the group.

Chapter 5

BECOMING A COMPASSIONATE CHRIST-FOLLOWER

Compassion lies at the heart of the authentic Christ-following life. Any spiritual experience – whether it be one of solitude and silence, prayer and fasting or worship and celebration – which does not result in a deeper concern for our suffering neighbour can hardly be called Christian. The crucial test of our relationship with the Holy One always involves the quality of our love for those around us. If our communion with God isolates us from the painful realities of our world, innoculates us against feeling the pain of our neighbours and leads us into an excessive preoccupation with our own well-being, it must be considered suspect. If, on the other hand, it finds expression in greater compassion and a willingness to show care, then it passes the test for genuineness.

This 'authenticity test' surfaces when we ponder upon the words and deeds of Jesus. Consider the parable of the Good Samaritan in this regard. A traveller on his way from Jerusalem to Jericho is mugged and left to die at the side of the road. Soon afterwards a priest comes by, and then a Levite, both of whom pass by without response. Finally a Samaritan stops, bandages the injured man's wounds, helps him onto his donkey and takes him to a nearby inn where he continues to take care of him. Jesus ends the parable with a straightforward challenge to the listening lawyer, 'Go and do likewise.' The central message of this parable is hard to miss. Participation in the kingdom requires that we share with others the same kind of compassion that we have received from God, and that we be humble enough to receive care from unlikely neighbours.

The deeds of Jesus also press home this message. Compassionate caring characterises his interactions with people, particularly his ministry to those in distress. We are told in the Gospels that it is with compassion that he touches the leper, responds to the hungry, opens the eyes of the blind and looks out upon the crowd who are like sheep without a shepherd (see Mk 1:41; 8:2; Mt 20:34; 9:36.) Scholars point out that the phrase used in these Gospel passages, 'to be moved with compassion', is used exclusively with reference to Jesus or his Father. The relevant Greek verb, *splangchnizomai*, reveals the incredible depths of this compassionate response in the Divine heart. In his reflections upon the noun from which this verb is derived, Henri Nouwen comments,

> The *splangchna* are the entrails of the body, or as we might say today, the guts. They are the place where our most intimate and intense emotions are located. They are the centre from which both passionate love and passionate hate grow. When the gospels speak about Jesus' compassion as his being moved in the entrails they are expressing something very deep and mysterious . . . When Jesus was moved to compassion, the source of all life trembled, the ground of all love burst open, and the abyss of God's immense, inexhaustible, and unfathomable tenderness revealed itself.[1]

Jesus' teaching and example shows clearly that he was 'walking, talking compassion'.[2] It follows that the life of discipleship, at its most genuine, involves becoming more compassionate. Such transformation comes about through the activity of the Holy Spirit working in us. We cannot, by our own efforts alone, change our hearts of stone into hearts of flesh. Nor can we study for a post-graduate degree in compassion! Compassion is a divine gift, made visible in those lives generously responsive to God and our neighbours. The first two ingredients of the pilgrimage experience – that is, encounter and reflection – are merely ways of getting ourselves ready for the breakthrough of love. Using excerpts from the testimonies of the pilgrims, together with some reflections upon Jesus' word and deeds, I will describe what this compassion might look like when the third ingredient of transformation takes place.

Awareness

Central to my experience of the Pilgrimage of Pain and Hope was that of deepened awareness. I became aware, for the first time in my life, of the tremendous pain experienced by the majority of our society – a pain so well camouflaged by the ruling government and manipulated media at the time. Encountering the pain and people involved firsthand – even though it was limited by time – brought home the reality far more deeply than watching a documentary on television. When leaving the places we visited, I knew I would never be the same again. To this day, even though much of the political horror has changed in South Africa, the Pilgrimage of Pain and Hope still remains embedded in my heart. The reality of people continuing to suffer daily due to poverty, crime, violence, sickness, injustice etc still challenges me to question its nature and to contribute in some small way towards its solution. Within my own vocation as a pastor, I see my calling as raising awareness, helping people to open their eyes to see the suffering around them, to see the presence of the risen Christ in those who suffer and to work in partnership with God in bringing wholeness and healing.

(A pilgrim)

Compassion, as this testimony suggests, flows from our becoming more aware of the human needs around us. Real awareness far exceeds the capacity of either information or rational analysis to effect lasting inner change. Before their participation in pilgrimage experience, many pilgrims already possess certain statistics surrounding the issues of poverty, homelessness, drug abuse and violence within the South African context. This knowledge, however, seldom engenders compassion. On the other hand, when these same pilgrims spend time with suffering people in these situations, share together a slice of life and reflect upon these encounters, a fresh awareness of these painful realities is generated. More often than not, it is the kind of awareness that responds and finds expression in a deeply felt compassion and caring.

Jesus' responses to those around him demonstrate further this connection between compassion and awareness. Study his relationships with people and you meet a man who comes across as being supremely aware and responsive. Consider briefly the following examples: he brings out into the open the critical thoughts of an antagonist, speaks exactly the right words that a paralysed man needs to hear, notices a desperate seeker after salvation hidden in a tree and hears the cry of a blind beggar above the din of a noisy crowd (see Lk 7:40–43; Mk 6:5; Lk 19:1–5; 18:35–40.) These incidents, and there are others like them, reveal the profound sensitivity of Jesus to each human being who crossed his path. Perhaps the one Gospel sentence that best communicates his awareness is one written in the second chapter of John's Gospel. There we read that Jesus '. . . needed no one to testify about anyone; for he himself knew what was in everyone' (Jn 2:25).

When our lives are touched by the Spirit we become more aware. As the Spirit filled Jesus and made him the most responsive and sensitive human being that ever lived, so the Spirit generates in us a similar current of awareness. In this way the Spirit gradually changes our hearts into the likeness of the compassionate Christ. On the pilgrimage experience I witness this pentecostal work in the lives of many pilgrims. Whenever their hearts are opened towards their suffering neighbour, in an attitude of openness and receptivity, they throb with new awareness. Indeed their caring responses underline the truth of John Taylor's powerful assertion,

> . . . I would say that God the Spirit is the unceasing animator and communicator, the inexhaustible source of insight, awareness, recognition and response.[3]

Another vital dimension of this compassionate awareness initiated by the Spirit of God, when understood within the Christian tradition, is the recognition of Christ in the last, the least and the lost. Recall that sentence spoken by Jesus in his parable on the Last Judgment, 'Truly I tell you, just as you did it to one of the least of these who are members of my family, *you did it to me*' (Mt 25:40, my italics). When the Holy Spirit breathes this sacramental awareness into our lives, as it happened for the pilgrim quoted, life-giving responses of compassionate caring are released. We realise that our care for those who suffer reveals the extent of our love for God and 'that Christ in his poor is neither a case nor a cause, but a mystery before whom we bow even while we serve'.[4] The more we enter this great mystery, the more we glimpse Christ reflected in the faces of those who suffer.

Mother Theresa's ministry on the streets of Calcutta witnessed powerfully to the compassionate consequences of recognising Christ in the least of his family. Having taken that Gospel sentence from the parable of the Last Judgment to heart, she went about serving the poor and destitute as if she was serving Christ. When questioned in a televison documentary by Malcolm Muggeridge about her motivations for doing what she did, this humble Christ-follower drew a distinction between her vocation and that of a social worker. When ministering to those who suffer, she and her team of nuns 'do it to a Person'. Without this interpretation of her actions, it is almost impossible to understand the devotion and sacrifice with which she gave herself to her suffering neighbour. She truly believed that in caring for the poorest of the poor, she was alleviating the on-going pain of Christ in our world.

Here is one experiment that may help you to open yourself more deeply to this Spirit-generated current of awareness and recognition between yourself and your suffering neighbour. Next time you find yourself in the midst of a crowd, ask God to deepen your awareness of those around you who may be carrying heavy burdens. Usually I remind myself that nearly every human being sits next to a pool of tears. Allow the presence of other people in all their inexhaustible mystery and burden and need to impinge upon your awareness. Recognise the people near you as living sacraments of the Divine Presence, each of them potential Christ-bearers to our world. Intercede for those who seem particularly troubled and down-hearted, and lift them inwardly into the healing light and love of God. Later in the day reflect upon your experiment in awareness and write out your responses in your pilgrim journal.

Empathy

> It was on the Pilgrimage of Pain and Hope that I was drawn out of my own little world into the bigger world of those in pain. At first I felt totally overwhelmed. After all what could I really do that would make a difference? But as the Pilgrimage progressed I slowly began to realise the importance of simply getting alongside suffering people and trying to understand life from their point of view. Even today when I meet someone in distress and pain, and there is little that I can do, I remind myself that I can try to be with him or her in what they are going through. This learning has made a great difference to the way I relate to others. When I am with people in pain I always try look past outward appearances and attempt to put myself in their place.
>
> (A pilgrim)

A second aspect of compassion, closely linked to new awareness, is empathy. The above quote from one pilgrim's testimony provides helpful clues into the rich meanings of this word. Empathy involves getting alongside others, being with them in whatever they are going through and putting ourselves in their place. At its simplest level, this usually means sitting down with a person, taking time to listen and trying our best to get his or her story right. More deeply however, empathy leads us into a close sharing of another's pain. We learn what it's like, in a small but significant way, to walk in our neighbour's

79

shoes. This shared experience of suffering comprises the heart of true compassion. Again Nouwen expresses it well,

> Compassion asks us to go where it hurts, to enter into places of pain, to share in brokenness, fear, confusion and anguish. Compassion challenges us to cry out with those in misery, to mourn with those who are lonely, to weep with those in tears. Compassion requires us to be weak with the weak, vulnerable with the vulnerable, and powerless with the powerless. Compassion means full immersion in the condition of being human.[5]

The shortest sentence in the Bible puts flesh on these words about empathy. In John chapter 11 we read about the dramatic events surrounding Lazarus' death and even-tual rising to new life. Tucked away amongst the details of this story are the two words, 'Jesus wept' (v 35). Meditating upon this incident I am struck by the fact that Jesus weeps immediately after witnessing the tears of Mary. This little detail suggests that Jesus was not so much crying for Lazarus (surely he knew that he would soon be raising him from the dead); but rather that his own heart had been deeply moved by the grief of those around him. Should there be some truth in this suggestion, the tears of Jesus in this scene show how completely God identifies with us in our suffering.

Frankly, I must confess that a part of me resists this chal-lenge of identifying with my suffering neighbour. The compassion that I see in the life of Jesus sometimes scares me. Perhaps it does you too. This could be why God's dealings with us include the rekindling of our longings to become more compassionate. While we can acquire skills that promote the growth of empathy, like learning to listen in an active way, in the final resort our hearts must be touched. And the good news that we have discovered from the pilgrimage experience is that, as we give ourselves to a real encounter with our suffering neighbour, the Spirit-breathed gift of compassion slowly takes shape in our hearts. We find our responses to suffering changing. Rather than wanting to avoid it at all costs, there is an ever-deepening desire to get alongside those who suffer, listen to their stories and be with them in their pain.

The value of this kind of empathy, from the perspective of those in pain, cannot be over-emphasised. My mind goes back to the frightening violence that preceded the first democratic elections in South Africa. During that time I found it deeply moving to witness on TV the presence of our church leaders amongst those who had suffered the loss of loved ones in the strife. Amidst so much pain and anguish there was little that these leaders could do. But they were *there*, offering their presence, getting alongside the grieving, listening to their words, sharing their pain and praying with them. I remember one mourner being interviewed saying quietly, 'It means everything to know that my bishop is with me at this terrible time.'

Action

The Pilgrimage of Pain and Hope has challenged me to become practically involved in the mission of Christ. I do not want to be a passive spectator any longer. The pilgrimage experience has taught me that the church is most effective when it is seen to be meeting the real needs of people. I want to be an active part of a Church that is relevant to the world outside its walls. I was also challenged to pursue my medical career in a way that will benefit most those on the underside of our society. I realised that it is not enough to be shocked or indignant at the life circumstances of people who suffer. If I am to follow the gospel way seriously I must be prepared to give my life in practical service as Christ gave his life for us.

(A pilgrim)

Compassion tries to respond practically in a situation of human suffering. Fifteen years after writing out the above reflections upon his pilgrimage experience, the pilgrim concerned continues to pour out his life in sacrificial service. Together with his wife and three children, he lives out his vocation as a doctor within a marginalised and disadvantaged community near Pretoria – training primary health-care workers, initiating self-employment opportunities for the unemployed, raising AIDS awareness amongst the school children and generally using his medical skills to make a creative difference in the lives of those around him. His example, hidden from the glare of the public spotlight, reminds me that compassion and practical action go together.

As usual Jesus leads the way in this regard. Compassion for him goes way beyond fleeting feelings of sympathy and pity; it expresses itself in practical actions aimed to relieve the pain and alienation of those who suffer. Gospel examples range from Jesus hugging a child, touching a leper, visiting the housebound, feeding the hungry, befriending the outcast, to miracles of him healing the sick and raising the dead. (See Mt 18:2; Mk 1:41; 1:30; Mt 15:32; Lk 19:6; Mt 11:4–5.) Passages like these show that compassion, in the way of Jesus, labours with the suffering for the sake of their greater well-being and wholeness. Learning to care as Jesus would, if he were in our place, means doing likewise. Controversial theologian Matthew Fox gets it right when he states,

Biblical compassion resists the sentimentalizing of compassion. In Biblical spirituality the works of mercy are *works* and the word for compassion in the Bible is more often employed as a verb than as a noun or an adjective. Compassion is about doing and relieving the pain of others, not merely emoting about it.[6]

Encountering those who are doing works of mercy encourages us to act similarly. Hence each Pilgrimage of Pain and Hope plans opportunities for its participants to meet with Christ-followers actively involved in compassionate ministry. On our most recent pilgrimage experience we spent time with a church-worker who ministers amongst the homeless, worked alongside volunteers serving in a soup-kitchen, spoke with a group of young people engaged in a year-long community service programme, listened to hospice workers describe their experiences with the dying and reflected with a missionary couple upon their church-planting efforts in an extremely disadvantaged community. These encounters with 'signs of hope' impact the pilgrims greatly. They learn that ordinary people can be wonderfully used by God to bring healing and wholeness, if only they are willing to act on behalf of those who suffer.

As followers of Christ, we are not left in the dark to wonder about the precise nature of these compassionate actions. Besides the example of his own life, Jesus also speaks about six ways in which authentic faith manifests itself. According to his parable on the Last Judgment, they are: feeding the hungry, quenching thirst, welcoming strangers, clothing the naked, visiting the sick and those in prison (Mt 25:35–36). Certainly this list was not meant to be exhaustive. These works of mercy are tied together by one common denominator – all of them are practical expressions of loving concern. Any action that leaves another person feeling more valued and loved, can be added. What matters is that, in our caring for others, we act appropriately.

In seeking to express my compassion in a more concrete manner, I find it helpful to review regularly my responses to those who suffer around me. Little growth in compassion occurs until we face honestly how little caring we usually do show. Once we realise the poverty of our loving, we can ask God to help us do better. New beginnings take place when we recognise that our acts of love are few, and then by resolving to find practical ways of expressing the compassion we feel in our hearts. Questions like these below keep me sensitive to the gospel challenge of living a compassionate life. You may find it useful to pause for a few moments and to consider them yourself.

- When did I last minister to the hungry, the thirsty, the homeless?
- How often have I gone out of my way to welcome strangers, particularly those who were not too interesting or attractive?
- When was the last time I visited a sick person, or someone who was bereaved, or one of the many depressed and despairing in my midst?
- Have I ever reached out in person to those in prison or someone who has recently been released?
- How do I show my care and concern on a daily basis to those around me, especially the suffering, broken and hurt?

In drawing attention to the active ingredient of compassion, I must introduce one cautionary note. Our best intentions on behalf of those who suffer go wrong when not attuned to their real needs. Too often, in our sincere desires to be compassionate Christ-followers, we engage in actions, unaware of their effect upon those being 'helped'. They may find our attentions intrusive or cloying, patronising, pretentious or even false. Our caring may also undermine the dignity and initiative of those suffering to do something themselves about their situation. Sometimes, as Sister Margaret Magdalen wisely comments, our '. . . *in*activity may well be the greatest mercy we could show . . .'[7] More, however, about this in the next chapter.

Compassion does not denote an extra 'commandment' for the really serious disciple; it describes the essence of the true Christ-following life. Spirituality that does not make us more caring cannot be called a gospel-spirituality. In this chapter I have tried to show that, in the light of Jesus' example and words, embarking along the compassionate way involves three crucial tasks: becoming aware of those who suffer, being with them in their pain and, where appropriate, acting together with them for the sake of their greater wholeness. Without the help and resources that come from the Spirit of God, we will not progress far along this road. Let us, therefore, pray that our hearts of stone become hearts of flesh.

Invitation to Pilgrimage

1. Describe *one* compassionate Christ-follower who has influenced your life.

2. Share your experience of the 'awareness exercise' suggested on page 78.

3. How do you resist the challenge to become a compassionate Christ-follower?

4. What did you learn from responding to the questions on the page 84?

5. What *one* practical step can you take during the next few days that will express your intention to grow in compassion.

Chapter 6

PREVENTING COMPASSION-FATIGUE

My own words surprised me. It was my Monday off and I was sitting with someone I trusted a great deal. For over eighteen months we had met together on a regular basis for me to talk about how my life was going. On this particular afternoon, as we sat opposite each other, a heavy weariness hung over me. The prospect of going to work the next day and facing my pastoral responsibilities filled me with dread. Inside I felt drained, dried-up and despairing. When I expressed my thoughts and feelings, it seemed that I was contradicting my deepest conviction about the Christ-following life. Struggling to keep my emotions under control, I said quietly, 'I really don't want to care for people anymore.'

I should not have been too surprised by my admission. For some years a number of internal 'indicator lights' had flashed on and off, cautioning me that I was on the edge of that condition known as compassion-fatigue. Instead of paying attention to these inner warnings, and revising the way I was living out my discipleship, I foolishly assumed that I could keep giving out without building into my life the necessary safeguards for my own well-being. Nor did I realise then, as I do now, that overcaring could be unhealthy. I needed to discover a better balance between the two extremes of self-centredness on the one hand and needless self-sacrifice on the other. Looking back as I write these words, I can see that three particular indicator lights warned me about the deteriorating condition of my soul.

First, there was the indicator light of the increasing exhaustion itself. With hindsight I realise how I allowed myself to become enmeshed in a downward spiral of caring activity. The dynamics of this vicious cycle were dangerously deceptive: when weary from being with those in need, I repeatedly sought to work through my tiredness by driving myself even harder. More often than not these extra caring efforts brought rewards of approval and appreciation which, by giving my flagging spirit a temporary high, camouflaged temporarily my worn-out condition. Thus I deceived myself into believing that I could keep on keeping on without replacing the energy used up in serving others.

Another indicator light was my resentment towards the constant demands made by those in need. Few other inner responses disturb Christ-followers more than this one, often leaving them feeling guilty, ashamed and unworthy. In my case, I hid my resentment behind a smiling face, judged myself harshly for feeling this way and ended up driving myself even harder in my efforts to show greater compassion. I became a 'happy servant' on the outside and a 'suffering martyr' on the inside. More recently I have recognised that these resentments do not always indicate selfishness; they sometimes also express the legitimate longings of our souls for nourishment and nurture. Acknowledging these soul-needs, and caring for them in appropriate ways, frees us for deeper self-giving.

A third indicator light was the lack of lightness and laughter in my life. Seeking to live the compassionate life became a grim and heavy-hearted enterprise. Seldom did I enjoy moments of glad celebration, spontaneous joy and carefree fun. Indeed, I felt that enjoying myself betrayed the pain and anguish of those suffering around me. Unlike the joyful Nazarene in whose footsteps I sought to follow, and who was accused of being a wine-bibber and a glutton, I rarely accepted invitations to enjoy a good party. Not only did I view life through sombre and dark spectacles, but even my picture of God assumed a rather gloomy countenance. Sadly, my life had lost that balance between the celebrative and serious sides so necessary for personal wholeness and generous loving.

I wonder if you can identify with any of these three warning signs? It's far better to recognise them early, and take the necessary preventative action, than to arrive in that desperate place where I found myself. Since acknowledging the extent of my own weariness on that Monday afternoon, I have begun to forge a more balanced way of life. With the help of trusted soul-friends, insights from Scripture and my closest family, I am doing three things that enable me to care in a healthier way. These are:

- becoming a compassionate neighbour to myself
- curbing tendencies towards compulsive caring
- developing a more celebrative lifestyle.

I outline them here with the hope that you find them meaningful in your own experience.

Becoming a Compassionate Neighbour to Myself

Christ-followers who take seriously the gospel's challenge to compassion frequently neglect to care for themselves. Whatever the reasons for this neglect are, and these may range from the fear of doing anything that looks selfish, always wanting to please others and needing to be needed to a sincere desire to put others first, not adequately caring for ourselves sets us up as prime candidates for compassion-fatigue. We can care overmuch. Accepting the fact that we can care for others only when we care for ourselves guards us against the dangers of over-caring. Morton Kelsey underlines this insight when he writes,

> Learning to be good Samaritans to ourselves is essential to becoming good Samaritans to others.[1]

Gradually, I have come to appreciate the wisdom of the above sentence. When we do not show compassion towards ourselves, our compassion for others becomes poisoned with all kinds of harmful toxins. However, once we learn to love ourselves as God does, the freer we become to pour out our lives in sacrificial self-giving, and to do so without resentment and heaviness of spirit. Having a proper love for ourselves, we can then forget ourselves, reach out to others and respond to their needs. Self-love and other-love are deeply bound together. Could this be the reason why Jesus reaffirmed the centuries-old Levitical command given to the Hebrew people as binding upon his followers. 'You shall love your neighbour as yourself' (Mt 22:39)?

Practically, how do we become compassionate neighbours to ourselves? There are several ways to begin. Here is a menu of possibilities worth exploring:

Take care of your body
In caring for others we use up a great deal of physical and mental energy. If these limited resources are not replenished, we run the risk of compassion-fatigue. I doubt whether we can fulfil our God-given callings to be compassionate human beings in bodies that are constantly

neglected and abused; therefore, we need to take care of them if we want to pursue the compassionate way. How we feed them, exercise them, relax them, listen to them and nourish them are matters relevant for faithful discipleship. When Francis of Assisi was dying, he was asked if he would have changed anything in his ministry. Significantly, he responded, 'I would have been more kind to my body.'

Recently I came across some well-documented research regarding the healthy care of the body. Involving careful investigations into the lives of nearly 7,000 adults, the study recommends seven basic rules of good health. If you are wanting to assess quickly whether or not you are taking care of your body, reflect upon your responses to the suggestions outlined. These were: do not smoke, drink alcohol only in moderation, maintain appropriate weight, eat breakfast, don't eat between meals, exercise regularly (brisk walking is especially recommended) and get 7 to 8 hours sleep daily.[2]

Do what you enjoy

Most people have some favourite spare-time activity. Whether it be working in the garden, walking in the countryside, playing sport, listening to music, reading for fun, developing a personal hobby, going to the movies or simply enjoying a leisurely bath, these activities possess wonderful resourcing potential. When we omit activities like these from our lives – as carers are prone to do – we end up living resentful, joyless and frazzled lives. On the other hand, taking time to enjoy them renews energy-levels, recharges inner batteries and fills our empty tanks. If we want to give ourselves in compassionate caring, there are few things more important than finding out what we enjoy doing – and doing it.

You can begin right now. Take a few moments to jot down all the activities that you enjoy. As outlined above, these activities don't need to be specifically religious. Select one which you can do in the next few days. Make sure you identify what *you*, and only *you*, would enjoy doing. This is a time for you to be yourself, to do just what you want to do, without worrying about pleasing others. Next, budget some time for this pleasurable thing. After you have done it, write out your feelings and thoughts about the exercise. Notice especially its effects upon your capacity to give yourself away in deeper loving and caring for others. Above all, discern the goodness of God in the good you were able to do for yourself, and give thanks for it.[3]

Process your own pain

Each of us sits next to a pool of tears.[4] While some of these pools are deeper than others, all of us have a pool of our own. These pools represent our grief about those experiences which have crushed our spirits, scarred our souls and crippled our relationships. Seeking to bring consolation and comfort to others in their pain, without giving attention to these painful memories, renders us highly vulnerable to compassion-fatigue. On the other hand, finding a human wailing wall where we bring our pain into speech renews our capacities to live and love more deeply. Besides experiencing the loving presence of God in the care and counsel of those who listen to us, we also find out that processing our own pain enables us the better to reach into the hearts of others who are in pain.

Permit me a brief word of testimony in this regard. Over the years numerous people have affirmed in my life the gift of listening. Large chunks of my daily time are spent offering a listening presence to people in pain. The flipside of this listening gift was, however, that I seldom spoke about my own pain. Bottled up feelings and emotions raged in my heart, longing for release. Some years ago I decided to find a safe place where I could share my heart. In the presence of a patient and skilled listener I gradually found the courage to express my inner anguish. It was a liberating, healing and humbling experience. This journey towards my own healing has not ended, but I do know today that without it I would not be in a position to care for others.

Curbing Tendencies Towards Compulsive Caring

Emphasising compassion as the central value of the Christ-following life, as I did in the previous chapter, brings with it one great danger. It can encourage us to become compulsive carers. In his reflections upon this possibility, Gerald May writes about 'addictive helpfulness' and invites his readers to identify their own automatic responses of showing compassion. He points out that we care compulsively when we ignore the tiny gap between feeling a person's pain and doing something for or to the suffering person. Consequently, when brought face to face with someone in need, we rush into the helpful role without first pausing to discern how best our compassion can be expressed. May describes how these addictions of helpfulness are triggered when we are faced with human need,

In a very computerlike way, our internal programs of what-to-do-in-a-situation-like-this are accessed and run. In a very uncomputerlike way, we don't even take the time to see which program is called for. There is no time. We must be about the business of being helpful.[5]

I witnessed an example of addictive helpfulness on a recent silent retreat. Early in the morning I came across a retreatant, whom I knew was going through a difficult time, sobbing before the crucifix in the chapel. Knowing that she was free to ask for companionship and prayer from myself if she wanted that, I left her alone. About an hour later I noticed another retreatant, arm around the distressed person, obviously seeking to bring comfort.

After the retreat ended I asked the retreatant who had been crying how she had found the silence. Her reply underlined how well-intentioned attempts at caring go badly astray when not attuned with what the one being 'helped' really needs or wants. She answered, 'Yesterday morning an old painful memory from childhood surfaced. I found myself grieving the loss in a way not experienced before. As I cried before the figure of the crucified Jesus I felt held in the loving presence of God. Unfortunately [here she named her "helper"] intruded into my silence. She insisted on sitting with me when all I needed was space. Her words and prayers really blocked the healing process. It took me almost the rest of the day to re-enter the deep place which I had touched before being interrupted.'

Not only do our addictions of helpfulness fail the person for whom we care, they also open the door to compassion-fatigue. When we disregard that vital space between feeling and response, we neglect the replenishing resources of the Spirit, exhaust ourselves in frantic do-gooding and burn out. This could be one reason why, when they write about compassion, seasoned associates of Jesus frequently mention the importance of attitudes like detachment, reticence, standing back, not doing too much, waiting, letting be and letting go. Such wisdom safeguards our caring from becoming intrusive, respects the space of our suffering neighbour and tops up our energy for continued self-giving. Curbing tendencies towards compulsive caring benefits, in other words, all parties involved in the helping relationship.

How do we begin to care less compulsively? First, we honour that gap between feeling care and compassion for someone and helping immediately. When we feel another person's pain, rather than leaping into any set or pre-determined active response, we acknowledge that we don't know exactly what this person needs. Our initial response must be our simple presence, listening as deeply as we can and getting alongside the suffering person. Inwardly, we direct a glance Godwards and ask, 'Lord, how would you have me respond here?' With this modest attitude we seek the whisperings of the Spirit, respect the mystery of our neighbour and practise the art of compassionate non-doing. Reflecting upon what happens in this gap between feeling and response, Sister Margaret Magdalen writes helpfully,

> For in that space we have the chance to listen to what [others] really need, to listen to the Lord whose compassion it is that we invite to flow through us, and to discern how *he* would want us to incarnate and express it.[6]

Secondly, we care less compulsively when we set limits to our caring. Compulsive carers feel obliged to respond to every request that comes along. Often promising to do more than they can possibly deliver, they do not set limits to their caring and so find themselves living amidst the debris of broken promises and disappointed expectations. Should you recognise yourself in these words, consider again the realism of Jesus who did not respond to every need, but rather singled out those he could help. Similarly, surrounded as we are by staggering human need, we cannot take all the world's pain upon our shoulders. Like Jesus, the best we can do is discern where we can express care and invest our energies there. In this way we guard ourselves against the dangers of addictive helpfulness, show respect for our own limitations and discover how to share wisely the love we have received from God.

Thirdly, we care less compulsively when we allow others to care for us. One of the hardest things for carers is to acknowledge their own neediness, ask for help and receive the compassion of loved ones and friends. I remember once sharing in a foot-washing ceremony during Holy Week. I found myself quite at home washing the feet of others. But when it came to having my feet washed I wanted to get up and leave the room. No wonder I found myself in my late forties struggling with the deadly effects of compassion-fatigue. An insidious pride had disabled me in receiving from others. Perhaps all who desire to become compassionate Christ-followers need to stick a new Beatitude on their fridges that reads, 'Blessed are those who are able to receive care from others, for they are able truly to care for others.'

Take a few moments to reflect upon the way you care for others. Three straightforward yes/no questions may aid your reflections. They are

- Do you usually rush into an active helpful role when faced with someone in need?
- Do you often experience weariness from taking on too many caring responsibilities?
- Do you normally struggle to share your needs with others?

Should you answer 'yes' to any of the above, you may

need to join me in curbing tendencies towards compulsive caring. Otherwise you could be heading for compassion-fatigue without even knowing it.

Developing a Celebrative Lifestyle

Joy is the primary antidote given to us by God for the prevention of compassion-fatigue. When it comes to our pursuing the path of compassionate discipleship, it constitutes our first line of defence against weariness, resentment and despondency. Scripture teaches us clearly that the joy of the Lord is our strength (Neh 8:10). Joy keeps us going, renews our energy and makes us strong. On the other hand, joylessness diminishes our capacity for self-giving and renders us vulnerable to those things that cause burn-out. It comes as little surprise, therefore, that the Apostle Paul wants joy to become an essential ingredient in the lives of all Christ-followers. Writing to the young New Testament churches he invites them repeatedly to rejoice, no matter what they are going through (see Phil 3:1; 4:4; 1 Thess 5:16.)

In our ravaged world, where evil appears to be stronger than good, some may protest against this insistence upon joy. Indeed, we may have every reason not to be full of joy; but we can *choose* a life of joy and do those things that open our lives to it. The fact that biblical writers frequently command us to be joyful implies that joy is both a gift and a duty. Joy does not happen automatically to us. In the breathtaking knowledge that the risen Christ has decisively overcome the powers of darkness and death, and that there is nothing that can ever separate us from God's loving presence, we have to choose joy. For some of us, especially if we have suffered greatly, this choice may well be the greatest challenge of our faith.

We open our lives to God's gift of joy by developing a celebrative lifestyle. In spite of the emphasis upon feast days and festivals in the Old Testament, and Jesus' first public miracle when he helped the wedding guests to celebrate by turning water into wine, celebration must rank as one of the most neglected and misunderstood disciplines of the spiritual life. Biblical writers assumed that times of feasting and festivity could build one's relationship with God just as much as regular times of solitude and prayer. Generally speaking, celebration involves coming together with God's people to eat and drink, sing and dance, pray and play and to share with each other stories of God's action and presence in our lives. Dallas Willard describes spiritual celebration in this way: 'We engage in celebration when we enjoy ourselves, our life, our world *in conjunction with* our faith and confidence in God's greatness, beauty and goodness.'[7]

My favourite description of celebration as a spiritual discipline occurs in the guidelines given in the fourteenth chapter of Deuteronomy. There the people of God are instructed to set apart a tithe of their yearly produce, transport it to Jerusalem and enjoy a feast in the presence of the Lord. If the distance proved too far for the goods to be taken to the great city, the tithe was to be converted into money and spent on '. . . whatever you wish – oxen, sheep, wine, strong drink, or whatever you desire. And you shall eat there in the presence of the LORD your God, you and your household rejoicing together' (v 26). Moreover, at the festival, outsiders were to be invited in to share in the feast. Imagine the joy as God's people came together and renewed their faith in this down-to-earth and pleasurable way.

While it would be wrong to use this Old Testament passage as an excuse for drunkenness, it does invite us to find earthy ways of celebrating together. Recently the small group to which I belong decided to experiment with the spiritual discipline of celebration. Together we planned an evening that enabled us all, both adults and children, to celebrate our belonging in Christ. It was a joy-filled night. Each family brought a plate of specially prepared eats, something to drink and their favourite music. The evening began with an ice-breaker in which everyone shared something good that had happened in their lives during the past week. We spent time worshipping together, clapping our hands and making a joyful noise as we sang some of our favourite spiritual songs. Around the candlelit table, against the background of gentle music, we ate and drank, told stories, shared snippets of news and enjoyed each other's company. The evening ended as we held hands together and gave thanks for the goodness of God. Afterwards I felt nourished in my faith, and strengthened to take up the responsibilities of my everyday life with greater love.

I hope that this has whetted your appetite for a more celebrative lifestyle. There are many small ways in which to begin. Allow mealtimes to become daily celebrations where everyone can share in conversation and laugh together; turn family events such as birthdays and anniversaries into occasions of fun and thanksgiving; wear clothes that make you feel happy to be alive; delight in the colours and textures of the natural world around you; spend leisure time relaxing with friends and family – and, as you do these things, enjoy the generous goodness of God. If you belong to a small group or local congregation, initiate discussions about how you can celebrate together as members of God's family. Take advantage of the great festivals of our faith – Christmas, Easter, Ascension and Pentecost – and build around them times of recollection and rejoicing. As you explore these possibilities, ponder the words of Jean Vanier,

> We must learn to celebrate. I say *learn* to celebrate, because celebration is not just a spontaneous event. We have to discover what celebration is. Our world doesn't know much about celebration. We know quite a bit about parties, where we are artificially stimulated with alcohol to have fun. We know what movies and distractions are. But do we know what celebration is? Do we know how to celebrate our togetherness, our being one body? Do we really know how to use all that is human and divine to celebrate together.[8]

Compassion-fatigue could be God's way of getting our attention when our caring goes awry. Certainly this was true for me. Thankfully, today I am more aware of the shadow side of compassion, and slowly discovering how to care in a more lifegiving way. As I become a compassionate neighbour to myself, curb my tendencies towards compulsive caring and develop a celebrative lifestyle, I find that I have more to give to others. And so, in your reaching out to your suffering neighbour, do not neglect your own needs, beware of addictive helpfulness and, above all, learn to celebrate.

Invitations to Pilgrimage

1. Can you describe a time of compassion-fatigue from your own experience?

2. In what *one* way can you better care for yourself?

3. Identify *one* symptom of addictive helpfulness in your life.

4. Do you enjoy God? If so, how?

5. Discuss possibilities for a group celebration and select one that you can pursue together in the near future.

Chapter 7

MAKING THE PILGRIMAGE EXPERIENCE PART OF OUR DAILY LIVES

After each Pilgrimage of Pain and Hope the pilgrims share their experiences in a variety of church settings. Not only do these testimony opportunities enable them to articulate what has taken place in their lives, their stories also encourage others to consider going on pilgrimage. I recall one young mother approaching me after the pilgrims spoke at an evening service. Their testimonies had affected her deeply, awakening a strong desire to go on the next pilgrimage. But with a demanding job to hold down, and two small children to raise, there was little hope that she could get away from home.

I still remember the question she asked, 'Is there any way in which I can go on pilgrimage right where I live?'

It was a good question. Already we have noted how the gospel invitation breathes the adventure of pilgrimage into the hearts of all who respond. When Jesus says, 'Follow me,' he calls each one of us to make our unique journey into the heart and life of God. The early Christ-followers understood this, and so described themselves as people of the Way. (See Acts 9:2; 18:25; 19:9,23; 22:4; 24:14,22.) Imagine how this self-description nurtured the pilgrimage metaphor in their hearts and minds. No longer were they drifters, unsure of who they were or where they were going. Now they saw themselves as pilgrims on a journey, travelling together along the discipleship road. And this is how God wants us to see ourselves, as we respond to the call of Christ. Alan Jones describes it well,

> The challenge of the gospel is, Will you allow your drifting to be consecrated into pilgrimage? Will you entertain the possibility that you matter, that you are here for a purpose, that you have a mission that no one else can fulfil?[1]

I hope that the central nature of this pilgrimage vocation has become clear in this book: as Christ-followers we are called to reflect his compassionate heart. Compassion and communion with a loving God belong together. Around this basic conviction the Pilgrimage of Pain and Hope has been presented as a means of spiritual formation and growth. By exposing participants to their suffering neighbour in personal encounter, drawing their attention to hope-creating responses and inviting their reflection upon what they experience, the pilgrimage experience provides a climate for discipleship growth that honours the centrality of compassion. It would be sad if only those able to leave domestic responsibilities could participate. I have learnt, however, that there are at least three ways in which we can become pilgrims in our daily lives.

Waiting Silently

We make the pilgrimage experience part of our daily lives by cultivating the practice of sitting still and waiting in expectant silence. Throughout this book my description of the Pilgrimage of Pain and Hope has been interspersed with references to solitude, silence and reflection. Unless we honour this 'inward' dimension of the pilgrimage experience, our growth into becoming compassionate Christ-followers degenerates into barren activism. Caring workaholics, while correcting what has been called a 'false inwardness', seldom make faithful pilgrims. Frantic do-gooding dulls our responses to the Divine Whisper, depletes our spiritual resources and often ends up in cynicism and despair. Aspiring pilgrims do well to heed the words of the psalmist, 'Be still before the LORD, and wait patiently for him' (Ps 37:7).

The Quakers demonstrate powerfully the relevance of this verse for all who care for others. Few groups have contributed as much to peace-making, a culture of non-violence, relief of suffering and the struggle for justice, as they have. Yet they cannot be accused of promoting a barren activism. Underpinning their vibrant social witness lies a highly effective and careful ritual for the practice of silent, expectant waiting. The other day, I was told that in front of the Friends' meeting house in Cambridge there is a sign which reads, 'Don't just do something . . . SIT!' In a contemporary church environment that encourages us all too often to over-extend ourselves in much doing, this sounds like timely advice. As Kenneth Leech wisely observes,

> The hyperactive person, whether community worker or pastor, who has not given time for inner stillness will soon communicate to others nothing more than his or her inner tiredness and exhaustion of spirit – not a very kind thing to do to people who have enough problems of their own.[2]

The biblical word 'rest' describes well this practice of sitting still in silent expectant waiting. 'Come to me, all you that are weary and are carrying heavy burdens,' says Jesus, 'and I will give you rest' (Mt 11:28). In this inner resting place we let go of our dependence upon words, lay aside our busy thoughts and put down our constant doing. Instead, we let God be God, and soak up his unconditional acceptance and merciful love. Persevering in this quiet way of prayer renews our spirits, refreshes our souls and replenishes our energies. Fresh streams of life-giving compassion begin to flow outwards from our depths. Having connected with the source of love in the still centre of our beings, we are empowered to care more deeply for others.

A delightful story about Abba Antony, one of the Desert Fathers, presses home the importance of this resting in God. One day a hunter came across Abba Antony and his brothers relaxing in the forest. The hunter expressed his surprise that so pious a man as Antony could sit and do nothing. Abba Antony invited the hunter to put an arrow in his bow and shoot it, which he did. Then the hermit asked him to shoot another, and another, and another. The hunter protested that if he continued shooting without a rest, the bow would break. Antony answered, 'So it is the same in the work of God. If we push ourselves beyond measure, we will break; it is right for us from time to time, to rest and relax our efforts.'[3] When we sit still in silent expectant waiting, we rest the bow and allow God to strengthen us for on-going ministry.

Given the unique way in which God deals with each of us, and our vastly different personalities, there will be a rich diversity in the ways we enter our inner rest in God's presence. Some find it helpful to choose a simple word or phrase, expressive of their longing for God, that they keep in their awareness. Examples range from single words like 'Abba', 'Jesus', 'Maranatha', to the well-known Jesus prayer, 'Lord Jesus Christ, Son of God, have mercy on me, a sinner'. Repeating our prayer-word or phrase for twenty minutes or so, and gently returning to it when our attention wanders, leads us into a restful place where we can attach ourselves more deeply to God. Others prefer to gaze at a picture or a symbol – a lighted candle, a crucifix, a single flower, an ancient icon – while they focus their hearts and minds on God. Whatever way used, the important challenge is to create a little pool of inner stillness in which to learn to '. . . know that I am God' (Ps 46:10).

Loving Special Neighbours

We make the pilgrimage experience part of our daily lives when we journey into deeper relationships with those closest to us. Our first priority in caring is always our special neighbours with whom we share our lives – our spouses, children, siblings, parents and close friends. Few things are more hypocritical than caring for distant neighbours at the expense of these family and friends. One sure sign that we need to stop and re-examine our priorities occurs when serving others spoils our intimate relationships. Dr Carl Jung once made a brief but telling comment on this particular issue. A friend was telling him about a certain man who was doing much good, and what a saint he was; Jung with a twinkle in his eye, responded, 'Oh, but I would want to meet his wife and children before I decided on his sainthood.'

Turning our intimate relationships into opportunities for pilgrimage does not happen automatically. The alarmingly high incidences of divorce, marital breakdown and relationship pain makes this clear. We struggle to love even those we have chosen. Furthermore, if we were raised in families characterised by constant tension, unresolved conflict, emotional coldness and physical abuse, our ability to relate warmly may be handicapped. The good news is that we can learn how to relate more intimately in our relationships. The pilgrimage experience, with its three ingredients of *Encounter – Reflection – Transformation*, has much to teach us. When we spend time with loved ones and reflect upon these encounters, our relationships become open to transformation and change. Notice the relevance of each ingredient for our journey into deeper relationships.

First, the pilgrimage experience underlines the importance of spending time with our special neighbours. Real encounter seldom happens in a hurry. If we really care, or want to care for someone close, then we need to spend unhurried time with that person alone. As I say to couples on their wedding day, 'Love is spelt TIME.' Recently I learnt that Susannah Wesley, the mother of John and Charles, had twenty children and yet managed to spend an hour a week alone with each of them. Eleven of the children became religious, political and literary figures in eighteenth-century England. Journeying into deeper relationships within our family and friendship circles requires this kind of time commitment. As Morton Kelsey points out, 'Love cannot be expressed without making time for the person whom we would love.'[4]

Secondly, the pilgrimage experience encourages reflection upon our responses in our relationships. Unless we stop and face honestly how we actually do relate, we will not grow in compassion. When we spend time with our special neighbours, and encounter them with their needs and shortcomings, deep emotional responses are evoked. Not only are our tendencies towards self-centredness exposed, we also receive glimpses of our potential for sacrificial loving. Taking time to reflect upon how we behave, sensitises us to these Spirit-generated awarenesses, facilitates better loving choices for the future, and helps us move towards becoming the person God wants us to be. Indeed, we seldom journey into deeper relationships until we face honestly how we do relate most of the time. In this reflective process two simple questions are helpful.

- How did I give and receive love today?
- How did I fail to give and receive love today?

Thirdly, the pilgrimage experience invites us to risk relating to our special neighbour in transformed ways. Possibilities for personal growth and on-going conversion abound in our close relationships, especially when we view them from a pilgrimage perspective. Through our reflections upon our ways of relating, God may call us to show our natural feelings of warmth and affection, or do some random acts of kindness, or give our partner more space, or stop our unhealthy withdrawal patterns, or learn how to ask for what we need. As we respond to these divine invitations, God inevitably empowers us with his gracious and constant companionship. In the final analysis, our growth in loving always comes as a gift and not as the result of our own efforts alone.

Recently I spent time counselling a young married couple. They asked for an appointment because they felt their marriage had become stagnant. 'Our relationship stopped growing on our wedding day,' explained the wife at our initial meeting, 'and we've been stuck ever since.' Together we explored ways of seeing marriage as an opportunity to go on pilgrimage into a deeper intimacy and friendship. They made regular appointments for time together alone, reflected daily on the two questions suggested above, and began viewing their marriage as God's means for their personal growth towards wholeness. In our final interview the husband remarked, 'It makes all the difference to see marriage, not as a destination, but as a journey.' They had become pilgrims in daily life!

Connecting with Suffering

We make the pilgrimage experience part of our daily lives by connecting with suffering. We have repeatedly noted that it is Christ through his Spirit who forms his compassionate heart in us. Transformation is the gift and work of God. Yet the moment we affirm this, we must not make the mistake of saying that there is nothing we can do. Indeed, it is only through a disciplined life that the transforming grace of God can flow into our lives. Traditionally, when Christian writers mention spiritual disciplines, their list has included those of solitude, prayer, Bible-reading, fasting, fellowship, worship and the like. In the light of the pilgrimage experience I want to emphasise one discipline seldom mentioned, and that is planned encounter with those who suffer in our midst.

I encourage you to begin simply. Commit yourself to spend a certain portion of your week, perhaps an hour, an afternoon or an evening, with someone who suffers. This person may be in prison, terminally ill, severely handicapped, economically impoverished or stuck in dark depression. As you plan to spend time with this person, remember the importance of cultivating a pilgrim attitude. (See Chapter 3.) Rather than rushing in with help or advice, the emphasis of your time together is being present, listening and becoming aware. Remind yourself that Christ promises to meet us in those who suffer. Do not underestimate what your simple presence may mean. After each visit, take time to reflect, write out your feelings and thoughts, and notice whether God is saying anything to you.

Like any other spiritual discipline, it's not always easy to stick with this commitment. Often we will find excuses to opt out, or to do something more 'productive' with our time. Nonetheless, as we persevere in this discipline, in the faith that God will meet us, we change. We find ourselves gradually becoming more responsive and aware, more sensitive to the pain that is around us. The Spirit of God is at work, opening our eyes, enlarging our hearts and making us into the compassionate people that we are meant to be. It may even happen that, through these planned exposures to people in pain, we hear God's call into a specific avenue of ministry. We discover that we are here for a purpose, and that we have a mission no one else can fulfil.

This happened for Hazel van Rensburg, a married mother with three sons who works as a freelance columnist. After attending a seminar where we explored this pilgrimage discipline of connecting with suffering, Hazel sought and received permission to visit women in her city's prison, on a weekly basis. It was the beginning of a profound inner and outer spiritual journey. Not only did Hazel discover what it means to really care, she found herself ministered to in remarkable ways. In an article she wrote for a national magazine she described her experiences. Here are a few brief extracts.

> 'Spend at least an hour a week with someone who suffers.' These were Reverend Trevor Hudson's closing words at a mission on the devotional life which I attended a few years ago. Words that for me would mark the beginning of a prison ministry which added a new dimension to my life as a Christian.

I remember clearly some of my expectations as I started out as a spiritual worker among the women prisoners in the city prison. I had aspirations of Bible study sessions which would revolutionise their lives. I visualised myself face to face with Jesus one day (trumpets sounding!) accompanied by a host of ex-prisoners who had met the Lord in prison.

Ironically, it was those very expectations which were to humble me: I wanted to do the work only the Holy Spirit could do, namely to change these women. I was to experience defeat and disappointment. I was to learn to persevere and to be patient. These women were running on empty. After six months my only achievement seemed to be that they now smiled at me when they saw me.

Of the many obstacles I would encounter was the uncomfortable feeling I had that the prisoners saw me as a kind of 'hanging judge' armed with a Bible and not to be trusted. Before I could do anything else, I had to show them that I really cared about them, that I was on their side, and that they mattered. I was not to judge and I was not to pry. They had to trust me.

Three months later I was to experience the glorious wonder of being ministered to while ministering. I was dealt a devastating blow when my younger brother died unexpectedly. I experienced grief I had never known. Consequently I did not feel inclined to visit the prison the next day, but somehow found myself there at the usual time.

I always started off my session with a caring question to each woman individually: 'What is in your heart today?' One young girl – barely 18 – shared the same agony every time: 'I just wish I could turn the clock back.'

But on that Sunday it was *my* heart that was so burdened that I shared my sorrow with them instead: 'I wasn't even able to say goodbye to him,' I confessed, the lump in my throat so thick that my words were hardly audible. I was overwhelmed by their love and compassion. No one had wept with me until then . . . These women, each with a criminal record, apparently the 'least' in society and who had themselves experienced the harsh bite of pain and lonely nights of grief, were the people used by God that Sunday afternoon to help lead me out of the valley of the shadow.

Finally

In a world which has become a global village, we are exposed to an indescribable amount of human misery. We cannot take responsibility for it all. We cannot feed all the hungry, visit all the sick, care for all the bereaved, befriend all the depressed and reach out to all the strangers. But we can, in silent expectant waiting, discern where the Lord wants us to reach out in compassion, and plan our time accordingly. If confined to home, we can always intercede or materially support ministry amongst the needy. And we can also phone someone who is hurting or send a card or answer a letter. In some specific way, each one of us can build the pilgrimage experience into our daily lives by connecting personally with suffering.

Our times cry out for a mass movement of compassion. This urgent need coincides with the goal of the Christ-following life for, unless our faith makes us compassionate, it can hardly be called Christian. Following Jesus means moving out of our privatised, isolated and self-enclosed worlds into a compassionate engagement with our suffering neighbour. As we open ourselves to the pilgrimage experience, either by going on a Pilgrimage of Pain and Hope or by building its key ingredients into our daily lives, we journey from self-centredness to compassion. May you and I become everyday pilgrims whom God can use to bring healing to our broken world.

Invitation to Pilgrimage

1. Would you see yourself as a drifter or a pilgrim?

2. Share your personal experience with stillness and silence.

3. Share *one* struggle that you have in loving your special neighbours.

4. Share *one* intention that you may have about connecting with suffering.

5. What are your plans to become a pilgrim in daily life?

Appendix

PLANNING A PILGRIMAGE OF PAIN AND HOPE IN THE LOCAL CONGREGATION

As a result of your reading this book you may want to plan a Pilgrimage of Pain and Hope in your own congregation. Here are ten 'travel tips' that you may find useful:

1. *Introduce the basic idea to the leadership of your local church.* Let the first chapter guide you in the preparation of your presentation. Make sure that you communicate clearly the basic aims and underlying philosophy of the pilgrimage experience. (See 'Essential Pilgrimage Ingredients' in Chapter 1.) Express your willingness to take responsibility for the planning process.

2. *Sound the call for the formation of a pilgrimage planning team.* Should the leadership give permission for a Pilgrimage of Pain and Hope, ask the wider congregation whether anyone would like to join you in further exploration and planning. Set up a date to meet with those who respond. Suggest at your first meeting that, in order to plan a local pilgrimage experience, it may be helpful to spend a few weeks going through this book together.

3. *Decide upon the length of your pilgrimage experience.* In

determining how long your pilgrimage will be, take into account the age group and circumstances of those you want to attract. Possibilities range from a week-long pilgrimage experience for younger people to a weekend or one-day event for those with families.

4. *Choose the places where you would like to go.* Possibilities include the following:

advice centre

awareness walk in a part of your town/city that is unfamiliar

home for the mentally handicapped

healing centre

hospice

inner city congregation

job creation projects

rehabilitation centre for recovering addicts

shelter for the homeless

street ministries

Add other possible venues from your knowledge of the local community. In drawing up your final itinerary plan one 'exposure event' per day.

5. *Liaise with 'bridge-person/s' already present within the place/s you intend to visit.* This particular person could be the co-ordinator of a service organisation, a community worker, a local pastor or priest, or a respected resident within a certain neighbourhood. When you make contact, introduce yourself and outline the purpose of your intended visit. Make it clear that you are coming to listen and learn. Discuss possibilities of conversation with those involved in active ministry, as well as with those who embody the 'human cry' of the community.

6. *Draw up a detailed daily itinerary.* Ensure that you set time aside each day for encounter, reflection, worship and fun.

Here is one example taken from our last pilgrimage when we visited a rehabilitation centre for young recovering addicts.

9.00 a.m.	Pilgrims meet together at the local church for 30 minutes of worship and prayer.
9.30 a.m.	Arrive at Rehabilitation Centre and have tea with co-ordinator.
10.00 a.m.	Co-ordinator shares the Centre's vision and explains the extent of the need.
11.30 a.m.	Pilgrims sit in on group session with some of the recovering addicts.
1.00 p.m.	Lunch with staff and residents.
2.00 p.m.	Pilgrims spend time individually with residents.
3.30 p.m.	Pilgrims return to local church and spend time reflecting upon the day. (See 'Keeping a Pilgrim Journal' and 'Structuring A Daily Solitude Time' in Chapter 4.)
4.30 p.m.	Group-sharing time. (See 'Sharing Our Experiences' in Chapter 4.)
6.00 p.m.	Light supper together at local shopping centre before pilgrims meet their hosts again at the local church.

7. *Form the pilgrim band that will be going on pilgrimage.* You can do this by personally inviting individuals, and also by putting out an advertising pamphlet in the local church or fellowship. Spend time with each applicant and make sure they understand the basic philosophy of the pilgrimage experience. Regarding the size of your group, aim for between ten and fifteen pilgrims.

8. *Plan a 'pilgrimage preparation day'.* Using the contents of Chapter 2, explore with the pilgrims the three ingredients of a pilgrim posture: learning to be present, learning to listen and learning to notice. You may find it helpful to do the exercises outlined in Chapter 2, as well as answer the questions listed under 'Invitations to Pilgrimage' at the end of that chapter.

9. *Examine the dynamics of re-entry.* Near the end of the pilgrimage experience, ask the pilgrims to list their concerns as they prepare to re-enter their home situations. Discuss these together and outline possibilities for on-going spiritual direction and pastoral support. Explore together what it may mean to make pilgrimage part of everyday life. (See Chapter 7.) Ask the pilgrims to write *one* paragraph about their pilgrimage experience, beginning with the words, 'On the Pilgrimage of Pain and Hope it has become clear to me that . . .'

10. *Provide testimony opportunities.* After the pilgrimage experience, allow the pilgrims to tell their stories amongst the wider congregation. Encourage the pilgrims to build their testimonies around the themes of awareness, empathy and action. (See examples in Chapter 5.) Besides encouraging others to consider going on a Pilgrimage of Pain and Hope, these testimonies help the pilgrims to integrate their own experiences more deeply.

Notes

Chapter 1

1. Trevor Hudson, *Christ-Following* (London: Hodder & Stoughton, 1996) p 94.

Chapter 2

1. Eugene Peterson, *A Long Obedience in the Same Direction* (Downers Grove, Illinois: Inter Varsity Press, 1980) p 12.
2. Douglas Steere, *Together in Solitude* (New York: Crossroad Publishers, 1982) p 176.
3. Catherine de Hueck Doherty, *Poustinia* (New York: Ave Maria Press, 1975) p 69.
4. Metropolitan Antony, *School for Prayer* (London: Daybreak) p 53.
5. Morton Kelsey, *Caring* (Mahwah, NJ: Paulist Press) p 72.
6. I have described this process of discernment at greater length in *Invitations to Abundant Life* (Cape Town: Struik, 1998) pp 46–48.

Chapter 3

1. Douglas Steere, *Gleanings* (Nashville, Tennessee: The Upper Room, 1986) p 67.
2. John Claypool, *Opening Blind Eyes* (Nashville, Tennessee: Abingdon Press, 1983) p 107.
3. I first came across this legend in Richard Foster's *Prayer* (London: Hodder & Stoughton, 1992) p 266.
4. Jean Vanier, *From Brokenness to Community* (Mahwah, N J: Paulist Press, 1992) p 19.
5. I learnt this prayer exercise from author Morton Kelsey.
6. This story is also recounted in my book *Christ-Following* (London: Hodder & Stoughton, 1996).

Chapter 4

1. Elizabeth O'Connor, *Letters to Scattered Pilgrims* (New York: Harper and Row, 1979) p 38.
2. I am in debt to Morton Kelsey for this insight. In his book *The Other Side of Silence* (London: SPCK, 1977) he distinguishes helpfully between a mature detachment that leads to a responsible living in the world and the kind that results in a pathological and distorted denial of life. (See pp 125–129.)
3. Catherine De Hueck Doherty, *Poustinia* (New York: Ava Maria Press, 1975) p 22.
4. Kenneth Leech, *True God* (London: Sheldon Press, 1985) p 119.
5. Quoted by Elizabeth O'Connor in her book, *The New Community* (New York: Harper and Row, 1976) p 109.

Chapter 5

1. Henri Nouwen, *Compassion* (New York: Doubleday & Company, 1982) p 16.
2. Sue Monk Kidd, *While the Heart Waits* (San Francisco: HarperCollins, 1990) p 202.
3. John V. Taylor, *A Matter of Life and Death* (London: SCM Press, 1986) p 10.
4. John V. Taylor, *The Go-Between God* (London: SCM Press, 1972) p 242.
5. Henri Nouwen, op. cit. p 4.
6. Matthew Fox, *A Spirituality Named Compassion* (Minneapolis, MN: Winston Press, 1979) p 7.
7. Sister Margaret Magdalen, *Furnace of the Heart* (London: Darton, Longman & Todd Ltd, 1998) p 94.

Chapter 6

1. Morton Kelsey, *Set Your Hearts on the Greatest Gift* (New York: New City Press, 1996) p 95.

2. I came across the 'Seven Basic Rules of Good Health' in *The Joy of Feeling Good* by William Miller (Minneapolis, MN: Augsburg Publishing House).

3. I have adapted this exercise from Wanda Nash's book *Turning the Downside Up* (London: HarperCollins) p 88.

4. It was in a conversation with Gordon Cosby that I first heard the phrase 'pool of tears'.

5. Gerald May, *The Awakened Heart* (New York: HarperCollins, 1991) p 237.

6. Sister Margaret Magdalen, *Furnace of the Heart* (London: Darton, Longman & Todd Ltd, 1998) p 92.

7. Dallas Willard, *The Spirit of the Disciplines* (London: Hodder & Stoughton, 1996).

8. Jean Vanier, *From Brokenness to Community* (Mahwah, NJ: Paulist Press, 1992) p 45.

Chapter 7

1. Alan Jones, *Passion for Pilgrimage* (San Francisco: Harper & Row, 1989) p 37.

2. Kenneth Leech, *The Eye of the Storm* (London: Darton, Longman & Todd, 1992) p 195.

3. I found this story in Sue Monk Kidd's *While the Heart Waits* (San Francisco: HarperCollins, 1990).

4. Morton Kelsey, *Caring* (Mahwah, NJ: Paulist Press, 1981).

The Exploring Prayer Series
Edited by Joyce Huggett

The Exploring Prayer series helps point the reader to God by drawing on the authors' own church and life experiences.

Angela Ashwin
PATTERNS NOT PADLOCKS
0 86347 088 3
Prayer for parents and all busy people.

James Borst
COMING TO GOD
0 86347 051 3
An introduction to contemplative prayer.

Ruth Fowke and Pam Dodson
CREATIVITY AND PRAYER
0 86347 278 8
How to use our creative gifts to enhance prayer.

Ruth Fowke
PERSONALITY AND PRAYER
0 86347 209 5
A doctor and counsellor tells how to find and extend the prayer style that suits our personalities.

THE EXPLORING PRAYER SERIES
Edited by Joyce Huggett

Trevor Hudson
COMPASSIONATE CARING
0 86347 295 8
Integrating caring and spirituality as a daily journey.

Joyce Huggett
FINDING GOD IN THE FAST LANE
0 86347 103 X
Encountering God despite everyday busy-ness.

Joyce Huggett
HEARING JESUS
0 86347 304 0
A fresh look at the parables of Jesus through a historical
and cultural context.

Joan Hutson
HEAL MY HEART O LORD
0 86347 213 3
Prayers and poems written for the broken-hearted.

Wendy Miller
SPIRITUAL FRIENDSHIP
0 86347 129 3
Building relationships through prayer and meditation.

THE EXPLORING PRAYER SERIES
Edited by Joyce Huggett

Michael Mitton
THE SOUNDS OF GOD
0 86347 067 X
Hearing the voice of God, drawn from the evangelical
and charismatic traditions.

Gerald O'Mahony
FINDING THE STILL POINT
0 86347 110 2
Help in understanding and governing mood swings.

Joyce Rupp
PRAYING OUR GOODBYES
0 86347 154 4
A helpful book about saying goodbye: to friends, jobs,
neighbours, or through bereavement to a loved one.